John, the Maverick Gospel

Robert Kysar

John Knox Press
ATLANTA

Scripture quotations are from *The New English Bible.*© The Delegates of the Oxford University Press and The Sydics of the Cambridge University Press, 1961, 1970. Reprinted by permission.

Acknowledgment is made for use of material from *The Foundations of New Testament Christology* by Reginald H. Fuller, copyright© 1965 Charles Scribner's Sons. Used by permission.

Library of Congress Cataloging in Publication Data

Kysar, Robert.
　John, the maverick Gospel

　Bibliography: p.
　Includes index.
　1. Bible. N.T. John—Criticism, interpretation, etc. I. Title.
BS2615.2.K93　　　226'.5'06　　　76-12393
ISBN 0-8042-0302-4

　10　9　8　7　6　5　4　3

Dedicated with gratitude to
Edward P. Blair

Preface

THIS BOOK IS ADDRESSED to the beginning student of the New Testament literature. It pretends to be neither technical nor scholarly, but it aspires to introduce the reader to the thought and symbolism of the Fourth Gospel as those matters are increasingly understood among the contemporary scholars and technicians of the New Testament. Thereby, I hope to lead the reader into the Fourth Gospel and bring him or her abreast of the way the Gospel is understood by a number of more advanced students.

Among the various introductions to the Fourth Gospel, therefore, this volume hopes to accomplish a number of distinctive things. *First*, I hope to stress the uniqueness of the Fourth Gospel among the literature of the early Christian movement. *Second*, and at the same time, I want to set the thought and symbolism of the Gospel in a much broader context, namely, that of the universal religious quest of humanity. The Gospel of John, this volume proposes, represents an exemplary piece of religious literature which poses questions which transcend Christianity alone to stand within the context of religion in general. The *third* peculiar feature of this introduction is its effort to keep the reader involved in the text of the Gospel itself. Too often reading an introduction to the New Testament or some specific portion of it draws the reader away from the document itself. So, the following pages are punctuated with insertions entitled "Reader's Preparation." These suggestions for reading in the Gospel itself will, I hope, make the task a triangular dialogue—a conversation among the Gospel, the reader, and the ideas of this book. The degree to which the reader is kept involved with the other two parties of this triad is the degree of the success of the book itself.

It has often been said that creativity is the art of forgetting the source of one's ideas. That is surely the case with the ideas of this book. While I have tried to acknowledge the sources of my ideas when I am conscious of them, I am sure that in many cases I have been negligent, and forgetfulness alone accounts for apparent creativity. Still, this sort of book should not be burdened with numerous footnotes. So, I ask the indulgence of my colleagues in Fourth Gospel criticism and ask the reader to take seriously the fact that the book is heavily indebted not only to the volumes listed in the bibliography but to a host of readings and conversations.

If I were to begin to acknowledge my indebtedness to persons, I would start with the mention of my students. The chapters of this book are the results of numerous efforts to interpret the Fourth Gospel to groups of beginning students—some young, some old, some within an academic setting, some within a church setting. I think of two groups in particular. One is the group of adults who gathered for a Lenten Bible Study in Center Church, New Haven, Connecticut, in 1974. It was in preparation for those sessions that these chapters first began to take shape. Then, they were further tested and revised by a group of enthusiastic, curious, and critical students in a class on the Fourth Gospel at Hamline University in the fall of 1974.

Certainly among the individuals to whom I am grateful always is Myrna, my wife. Her theological perception and her understanding of human nature have taught me a great many things, and without her encouragement of my literary efforts this volume would not exist. Another individual who has shaped the whole of my career is Edward P. Blair, Professor Emeritus of Garrett Evangelical Theological Seminary. It is with gratitude for all that he taught me that I dedicate this volume to him.

Contents

Introduction

THERE IS A DELIGHTFUL LITTLE FILM about a small boy who learned to walk on his hands instead of his feet. The story is done in animation and stresses the pressures toward conformity in our society. The little boy's strange behavior had the most pleasant results for him. Walking on his hands gave him a radically different perspective on the world. He could smell the fragrance of the flowers without bending down. He was close to the earth so that he could see vividly the beauty of grass, and he met the butterfly eyeball to eyeball as it skimmed along the ground. His parents, on the other hand, were deeply distressed! Their daring little boy was a misfit! And so they took him first to a medical doctor, then a psychiatrist, and then a social worker. All of the newest theories were employed to change the little boy's behavior. Gradually he was made to learn to walk like all other humans—on his feet. The parents were relieved; the doctors, social workers, and others who had helped were proud of their success. But now the little boy began to see the world as others saw it: dirty, ugly, polluted, and filled with persons obediently doing what was expected of them. His short-lived posture which enabled him to appreciate more easily the beauty of the world was ended. Now he was like everyone else!

The little parable illustrates the manner in which conformity is given high priority in our society. But it also suggests the way in which non-conformist positions in religion are made to fit into the mainstream of traditional thought. Religions must by their nature be homogeneous, lest their claim to the truth about human existence and the cosmos seem compromised. Sometimes a religious tradition is flexible enough that it somehow manages to encompass variations of interpretation within its midst. Hinduism is an example. Other religious traditions more characteristically tend to abort those movements which are heterodox. The history of Christianity is dotted with such events, most especially the fragmentation of Protestantism. One way or another, religions must deal with the non-conformists—those who appear to walk on their hands.

Early Christianity soon developed a tendency to view its origins from a single perspective. The belief that the earliest years of Christianity saw the emergence of one harmonious community was very quickly held. Read the account of the earliest church in the Acts of the Apostles and then compare it with the letters of the apostle Paul. It is obvious that already the author of the Acts was presenting a view of the earliest church which smoothed out the differences among the first believers. By 80-90 A.D. Luke was already attempting to propagate an understanding of the earliest church as having been without significant rift! Paul's letters, on the other hand, would seem to suggest that there were important differences at least between him and certain other Christian leaders. (That is especially evident in Galatians.)

It is not surprising, therefore, that the history of the interpretation of the Fourth Gospel has tended to stress its similarities with the other three canonical Gospels. The so-called "harmonies of the Gospels" popular in previous centuries struggled to fit the account of the ministry of Jesus found in the Gospel of John into the pattern presented by the first three Gospels. For example, Jesus is represented as cleansing the temple early in his ministry in the Fourth Gospel (2:13-22) but in the very final week of his ministry in the other Gospels (Matthew 21:12-13; Mark 11:15-19; Luke 19:45-46). The harmonizers solved the problem with the suggestion that Jesus cleansed the temple not once but twice! Let's all walk on our feet!

Given this tendency to harmonize the four Gospels, the uniqueness of each of the Gospels is overlooked. Particularly is this true of the Fourth Gospel. To make it conform with the first three Gospels is to rob it of its vitality and its contribution to our understanding of the origins of the Christian movement. The very title given now to the first three Gospels among students of the New Testament stresses the peculiarity of the fourth. They are called the *synoptic* Gospels. This means that they have a common point-of-view, that they see their subject in a similar fashion. The Fourth Gospel is not synoptic, then, but sees its subject in a way which stands quite apart from its three colleagues in the Christian canon. If you will, the Fourth Gospel is a maverick among the Gospels. It runs free of the perspective presented in Matthew, Mark and Luke. It is the non-conformist Gospel of the bunch. No wonder that many of the heretical movements in the history of the Christian church have used the Gospel of John as their authority in the New Testament.

What I want to stress at the beginning of this introduction to the religious thought of the Fourth Gospel is that it represents a unique form of early Christian thought. It is a heterodox form of Christianity, at least when compared with other literature in the New Testament. Let us then examine a number of preliminary matters about the Fourth Gospel. And as we do so, let us keep this assertion in mind, namely, that in the Fourth Gospel we have a maverick form of early Christian thought. Those issues which we must briefly look at are two: (a) The relationship of the Fourth Gospel and the Synoptics; (b) A series of matters, including the purpose of the Fourth Gospel, its date and destination, and its historical environment. What follows are really assertions of my opinion on these matters. They will supply the context within which we will go on to examine the religious thought of the Gospel. You are invited to test my opinions with the evidence in the Gospel itself as we proceed.

Reader's Preparation: Read quickly through the Fourth Gospel. Note its language and style. Get in mind a general outline of the book.

A. THE RELATIONSHIP BETWEEN THE FOURTH GOSPEL AND THE SYNOPTICS

Since I want to stress the peculiarities of the Fourth Gospel as compared with the Synoptics, we will examine first of all the *differences* between them. Having done so, we shall point out the similarities between it and the Synoptics.

Reader's Preparation: (1) Read Matthew 1-2, Mark 1:1-11, and Luke 1-2 and compare it with John 1:1-18. (2) Read and compare Luke 11:14-20 and John 5:10-24. (3) Read one of the parables from the synoptic Gospels (e.g., Luke 10:29-37) and one of the allegorical speeches in John (e.g., 10:1-18). (4) Compare Matthew 6 with John 8. (5) Compare Matthew 9:18-26 with John 11.

The reader gets no further than the introductory chapters of the Gospels before the uniqueness of the Fourth Gospel stands out. Matthew and Luke each in his own way presents the reader with an account of the birth of Jesus and a genealogy. Mark dives right into the ministry of Jesus itself; he has no account of the birth of Jesus, but begins with the preaching of John the Baptist. The fourth evangelist, like Matthew and Luke, has a preface to the account of the preaching of the Baptist, but what a distinctive preface it is! No birth account! No virgin conception! No genealogy! Rather, the reader steps onto the stage of the *cosmos*. We begin "In the beginning." The attention is upon the "Word" and its activity. It is with God in the beginning: it participates in creation; it becomes flesh. The Baptist is introduced as one distinct from this incarnate word but as one who bears witness to it.

The reader is struck then by the cosmic setting of the Gospel. If Matthew and Luke stress the role of God in the origin of the subject of their Gospels, John stresses the eternal status of that subject. Jesus is not born—not even by the intervention of the Holy Spirit in a wondrous way. He has always existed. He is but the incarnate appearance of the eternal Word. Hence, the Fourth Gospel begins by making the highest possible claim for the person of Jesus—his divine nature.

The prologue of the Gospel (1:1-18) suggests, too, the differences of style and language between the fourth and the synoptic Gospels. Did you note the use of the words "life," "light," "darkness," "true," "world," "Father," and "son"? These are among some of the favorite expressions of the writer of the Fourth Gospel. Others are "knowing," "seeing," and "the Jews." He likes to have Jesus introduce his utterances with the expression, "Amen, amen" (translated, for instance, "In very truth"). Moreover, he has a series of emphatic "I am" sayings attributed to Jesus. (We will examine these in the following chapter.) While most of these terms can be found in the synoptic Gospels, they do not play such a featured role in the sayings of Jesus there. For instance, those scholars who have time to do so have counted the number of times Jesus is made to refer to God as Father in the synoptic Gospels and in the Fourth Gospel. Their findings are instructive: Father is used of God 64 times in the first three Gospels and 120 times in the Fourth Gospel.

Moreover, some of the more prominent terms in the synoptic Gospels are relegated a secondary role in John. "The kingdom of God" ("Kingdom of Heaven" as Matthew would have it), "repent," "apostles," "scribes," "Pharisees," "tax collectors," "adultery," "demon," and "inherit" are examples of often used words in the Synoptics found rarely if at all in the Fourth Gospel.

What may we conclude? Simply that the writer of the Fourth Gospel has a unique vocabulary. It is one that is rich and profound, but above all distinctive.

A third kind of distinctiveness about the Fourth Gospel we might call chronological (and order of events). An apparently small detail which might have great significance is the number of Passover references. In the synoptic Gospels there is but one reference to the Passover celebration. That is the occasion of Jesus' trip to Jerusalem which culminates in his arrest, trial, and crucifixion. In the Fourth Gospel, however, there are three Passover occasions cited (2:13; 6:4; and 11:55). The result of these chronological references is that, according to John, Jesus spent more of his ministry in Judea than in Galilee. This is quite in contrast with the Synoptics where Jesus spends the bulk of his time in Galilee and travels on only one occasion to Jerusalem for the celebration of Israel's escape from bondage.

Perhaps more important than the simple difference of geography is the fact that his change of the locale of Jesus' ministry in the Gospel of John means a radical departure from the basic pattern of the synoptic Gospels. That basic pattern (perhaps originating with Mark and followed by Matthew and Luke) divides the ministry of Jesus into two parts—a Galilean and a Judean ministry. John in no way adheres to such a pattern and has Jesus freely moving back and forth between the two areas.

If we are to take John's chronology quite literally, it means that he conceived of Jesus' ministry as spanning three years. The synoptic chronology would suggest that Jesus' ministry was encompassed within one year. But more likely is the possibility that the chronology of the Fourth Gospel has theological significance. John may want to stress the Passover in relation to Jesus' ministry, because he finds in that ministry the new exodus and in Jesus the opportunity for a new Passover celebration. But such suggestions must await further exploration.

Another difference in chronology is evident to the careful reader. According to the Synoptics, Jesus' last meal with his disciples before his arrest, trials, and eventual crucifixion occurs at the very time other Jews are celebrating the Passover meal. But in the Fourth Gospel that last meal occurs in effect twenty-four hours earlier, and his crucifixion and burial are completed before the Passover meal. The relationship between these events in Jesus' life and the Passover observance appears this way in the Synoptics and John:

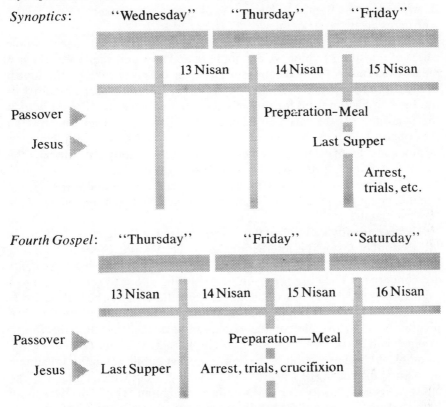

Synoptics: "Wednesday" "Thursday" "Friday"

13 Nisan 14 Nisan 15 Nisan

Passover ▶ Preparation-Meal

Jesus ▶ Last Supper

Arrest, trials, etc.

Fourth Gospel: "Thursday" "Friday" "Saturday"

13 Nisan 14 Nisan 15 Nisan 16 Nisan

Passover ▶ Preparation—Meal

Jesus ▶ Last Supper Arrest, trials, crucifixion

Let's note a couple of things about this comparison before we dismiss too lightly this apparently insignificant deviation between the Gospels. First, the implication of the synoptic account is that the last supper with the disciples was a Passover celebration. The so-called institution of the sacrament of the Last Supper is then to be understood in the context of Jewish Passover observance. But the Fourth Gospel loses that significant association of the Last Supper and the Passover by placing the event one day earlier in the career of Jesus. So, in the Fourth Gospel there is no formal institution of the Last Supper (see chapter four) and, further, the occasion of the last meal has no clear affiliations with Passover.

Second, note the results, however, of the deviation in John for the relationship of the crucifixion of Jesus to the Passover. According to the Fourth Gospel, Jesus was crucified at the very time the preparation for the Passover meal was being made. That preparation involved, of course, the slaughter of the Passover lambs and their preparation for the subsequent meal. Jesus is slain at the same time the Passover lambs are slain! A coincidence? Or, are we to understand the parallel to be a deliberate allusion to the nature of Jesus' death? Are we to associate this parallel with the witness of the Baptist to Jesus, "Look, there is the Lamb of God; it is he who takes away the sin of the world" (1:29 and 36)?

Actually this slight variation of the dating of the last meal raises a whole series of questions (which we cannot here and now consider): Was the last meal Jesus had with his disciples a Passover observance? Did the fourth evangelist employ a Jewish calendar different from that of the majority of the Jews of his time and for that reason date the occasion differently than the Synoptics? Is the variation an intentional historical observation on the part of the fourth evangelist, or a casual slip? Did he intend a symbolic significance to his dating? Which of the two accounts (if either)—the Synoptics or the Fourth Gospel—is historically accurate?

Could it be that the fourth evangelist intended us to find a theological significance in the parallel between Jesus' crucifixion and the killing of the Passover lamb?

We have already mentioned the different place of the temple cleansing in the account of Jesus. It is interesting that in the synoptic Gospels that event is the last public act of Jesus. It is the "last straw" so far as his opponents are concerned. They are represented as setting about to seek a means of ridding themselves of this troublemaker immediately *after* he had done this brazen deed (Mark 11:18). So, in the Synoptics the temple cleansing is the pivotal event in the plot of the last days of Jesus' life. But the fourth evangelist has the event as the *first* public act of Jesus (excluding the wedding at Cana as a public occasion). The last public act in the Johannine account is the raising of Lazarus, and it is that event which stimulates the antagonists of Jesus to seek ways of destroying him (11:47-54). We cannot here explore the reasons for the difference except to note that again there is a symbolic role given the temple cleansing in the Fourth Gospel. Standing as it does at the beginning of Jesus' ministry, it seems to suggest that his ministry was in general designed to cleanse Judaism.

Enough has been said of the chronological differences between the Synoptics and John. Let us consider next the difference in the portrayal of Jesus in the two. First, we must note the silence of the Fourth Gospel with regard to a series of very important events in the synoptic scheme of things. Missing from the Fourth Gospel are the following: (1) Jesus' baptism at the hands of John the Baptist. (The Baptist is nothing more or less than a witness to the Christ.) (2) The temptation in the wilderness. (Jesus is never subjected to temptation in the Fourth Gospel; he seems far above such difficulties.) (3) The confession of Caesarea Philippi where Jesus evokes from Peter the declaration, "You are the Messiah." (Mark 8:29) (See however John 6:66-71.) (4) The transfiguration. (5) The agonizing struggle in the garden of Gethsemane. (6) The institution of the Last Supper. (7) The cry of dereliction from the cross ("My God, my God, why hast thou forsaken me?''—Mark 15:34-35 and Matthew 27:46—the only words of Jesus from the cross recorded in two Gospels.)

On the other hand, note a few examples of events found in the Fourth Gospel about which we hear nothing in the Synoptics: (1) The wedding at Cana. (2) The conversation with Nicodemus. (3) The encounter with the woman of Samaria. (4) The raising of Lazarus. (5) The washing of the feet of the disciples.

There are related deviations. In the Synoptics the ministry of Jesus does not begin until John the Baptist is arrested (Mark 1:14; Matthew 4:12; Luke 3:19-20). But in the Fourth Gospel Jesus is made to have a concurrent ministry with that of the Baptist. In stark contrast to the gospel of Luke, especially, Jesus does not have to pray, according to the Fourth Gospel (11:41-42). In the Synoptics we get the picture of Jesus, the rabbi. He argues with the teachers of the day over such issues as the observance of the Sabbath (Mark 2:23-28), fasting (Mark 2:18-22), and divorce (Matthew 19:3-9). The impression one gains is that of a teacher and interpreter of the Old Testament—although a radical one, to be sure. But his rabbinic characteristic is missing in the Fourth Gospel. Jesus has controversy with the leaders of Judaism, granted, but the controversy is over the issue of Jesus' own identity, not the interpretation of Torah. Furthermore, the synoptic Gospels (especially Mark) contain the fascinating feature of what has been called the "messianic secret." For the most part it has to do with Jesus' practice of exhorting those whom he has healed to remain silent and tell no one of Jesus' wonders (e.g., Mark 1:43-44). That whole matter is entirely missing in the Fourth Gospel, and the only thing which we might claim to be comparable is the manner in which Jesus is constantly misunderstood by those around him (e.g., 8:27).

The impression which these differences leaves on the reader is that the johannine Jesus is clearly a divine, heavenly being. The Jesus of the Fourth Gospel is openly and clearly "extra-human." He knows who he is and speaks constantly of it. If the Synoptics hint at any sort of hesitancy on the part of Jesus in identifying himself, the Fourth Gospel has obliterated that hesitancy. Moreover, Jesus' extraordinary powers are emphasized in the Fourth Gospel. We will see this with regard to the wondrous acts attributed to him when we discuss that subject below. For now it suffices to observe that this johannine portrait of Jesus is through and through a marvelous one! This man does not have to pray. He knows the thoughts of others before they speak (1:47 and 2:25). He walks through the midst of a hostile crowd without a hand laid on him, because "his hour had not yet come" (7:30 and 8:20). I do not want to say that the portrait of Jesus in the synoptic Gospels lacks an extra-human dimension; for that is surely not the case. Nor do I want to say that the Jesus of the johannine Gospel is pure spirit with no human dimension, for that is surely not the case (e.g., 11:35; 19:28; 21:9-13). It is true that the johannine Jesus is extra-human in a manner which exceeds that feature as it is represented in the synoptic Gospels.

The speeches of Jesus in the Synoptics and Fourth Gospel offer another contrasting feature of the two portrayals of the Galilean. I want to generalize from evidence of the kind you sampled in reading the speeches of Jesus from the Synoptics and John. The speeches of Jesus in the synoptic Gospels seem to be of two kinds: short, pithy sayings or parables. The extended speeches in the Synoptics (e.g., the Sermon on the Mount in Matthew 5-7) clearly appear to be collections of short sayings. The parables are sometimes extended, sometimes brief. Sometimes they are story parables (e.g. Luke 15:3-32), sometimes simple comparisons (e.g., Matthew 5:13).

In John the words of Jesus are quite different. First, the story parable is entirely missing. There are comparisons made, but they take on the form of elaborate allegories and lose the simplicity which their counterparts in the Synoptics have. Moreover, the subject shifts. The subject of the allegorical speeches in John is always the same—the identity of Jesus (e.g., 8:12, 10:1-18; 15:1-10). The subject of the parables in the Synoptics, in contrast, is consistently the kingdom of God (e.g., Matthew 25:1). Those short, pithy sayings of Jesus in the Synoptics? They too are missing, for the most part. Instead, Jesus' speeches are long, extended discourses—perhaps even wearisome in their length. Jesus is made to go on and on (like a college professor, one might insert). From the point-of-view of good communication, he is prone to repetition and obscurity. The logic of these discourses is not at all clear. If one wanted to speak of them as logical at all, it would have to be said their logic is like a spiral rather than a lineal development. As with the parabolic comparisons, the discourses of Jesus have but one subject— his identity, his origin, his relation with the Father. Finally, I should add that in the Synoptics many of those short, pithy sayings are found at the conclusion of brief encounters and discussions (usually with the opponents of Jesus). An example is the famous saying about the Sabbath day (Mark 2:23-28). There is a dialogical character to many of the discourses in the Gospel of John. But the partners in the dialogue with Jesus do little more than mutter their disagreement and entirely and curiously misunderstand him. This simply occasions Jesus' taking up the subject again to go on at some further length.

The discourses of Jesus in the Fourth Gospel suggest a different understanding of the Christ figure and a different view of his teaching. He is above all the revealer whose words are the essential knowledge needed for human salvation. He stands apart from human teachers, for he is the proclaimer whose proclamation is one with his person. That is, the revelation contained in the words of johannine Jesus has to do with the identity of the proclaimer.

We are led finally to a look at the differences between the Synoptics and the Fourth Gospel in their representation of the wondrous works of Jesus. There are four observations to be made. First, the most common form of wondrous deed attributed to Jesus in the synoptic Gospels is the exorcism —driving out demons and overcoming the demon possession of persons. Exorcisms dominate the wondrous works of Jesus especially in Mark (e.g. 1:23-28; 5:1-10; 7:25-30; 9:19-27). But, oddly enough, they are conspicuous only by their absence in the Gospel of John.

Second, it is a fair generalization to say that the marvelous quality of Jesus' acts are heightened in the Fourth Gospel. The healings accomplished by the johannine Jesus are even more remarkable than those claimed by the Synoptics. The illnesses cured are longer. Often they are infirmities known by the patient from birth. There is possibly a sense in which the wondrous deeds done in relationship to nature are more extreme. That is, in those cases in which Jesus works marvelously with nature as opposed to persons, those acts are more startling. Examples include the transformation of water into wine (John 2:1-10) and the extraordinary catch of fish (John 21:1-11).

But most telling is the comparison of the raising of persons from the dead. You were asked to compare the account of the raising of the daughter of the ruler in Matthew 9 with the resurrection of Lazarus in John 11. In the matthean account the girl's condition is questionable. Jesus insists, "The girl is not dead: she is asleep." (v. 24). This is in spite of the father's statement that she is dead (v. 18). With Lazarus (John 11) there is no question about it—he is dead. He has been in the grave four days (v. 39). The suggestion this fact would have to the original readers was that his spirit (his life-breath) had departed. (Jewish thought of the day would seem to hold that the life spirit of the deceased hovered about the grave for three days before departing entirely.) The mourners are reluctant to remove the stone from the grave because the body has already begun to decompose and the odor would be frightful. Lazarus is dead—no question about it. Hence, this is no mere resuscitation as might be the case in the synoptic stories. This is a genuine resurrection from the dead.

Our third observation is a way of qualifying the emphasis upon the extension of the wondrous quality of the acts of Jesus. For in spite of what we have just said, it must be pointed out that the number of wondrous deeds attributed to Jesus in the Fourth Gospel is significantly fewer than in the Synoptics. The wonders of Jesus dominate the Gospel of Mark. But the Fourth Gospel records only seven (or eight) wondrous works:

1. The Marriage at Cana (2:1-11)
2. Healing of the Nobleman's Son (4:46-54)
3. Healing at the Pool of Bethesda (5:2-9)
4. The Feeding of the Multitude (6:1-15)
5. Walking on the Water (6:16-21)
6. Healing of the Man Blind from Birth (9:1-7)
7. Raising of Lazarus (11)
8. The Miraculous Catch of Fish (21:1-7)

Chapter 21 is regarded by most as a later addition to the Gospel. Hence we may say the Gospel originally contained only seven accounts of marvelous deeds. Few but forceful they are!

The exorcisms common to the Synoptics are strikingly missing in John. The wondrous acts are heightened in their marvelous quality, although few in number. But finally the wondrous deeds of Jesus in the Fourth Gospel clearly have a different function than their counterparts in the first three Gospels. As you read in Luke, the casting out of demons was significant for it signaled the advent of the kingdom of God (11:14-20). Set as they are in the context of Jesus' proclamation of the beginning of the kingdom of God (Mark 1:14), the wonders done by the synoptic Jesus point to the reality of that newly asserted reign of God in the world. These deeds point beyond Jesus, one might say, to the presence of the kingdom inaugurated by his ministry. Not so with the wonders performed by the johannine Jesus. They point not to the kingdom of God. (There is, as I have said, little talk of the kingdom at all in the Fourth Gospel.) Rather they point to the identity of the performer himself. They are in fact called "signs" in a number of passages (e.g., 2:11; 4:54; and 20:30-31). They are understood as indications of the true identity of the performer. They are intended to evoke a believing response to the claims of the one who does them. Thus the wonders are given a revelatory character along with the words of Jesus: They reveal the truth about the identity of the revealer. There are more complex problems associated with the function of the signs and works of Jesus in the Fourth Gospel which must occupy us later. For now we should note only the sense in which the wondrous acts of Jesus are treated so differently in the fourth than in the synoptic Gospels.

So much for the differences between the Fourth Gospel and the Synoptics. That is half of the story (the larger "half," I believe). The other half is the sense in which there are striking *similarities* between the maverick Gospel and its three colleagues. I will only suggest a few examples of the similarities—enough, I hope, to pose more sharply the problem of determining the relationship between the two.

The similarity between the Fourth Gospel and the Synoptics which is the most obvious is their accounts of the passion story. With the Synoptics, the Fourth Gospel records the same basic story of Jesus' separation from the disciples, the arrest, trial before both a religious body and the ruling political chief, the execution, burial, and finally the resurrection. To be sure, each of the Gospels has its own peculiarity somewhere in the account (e.g., Luke reports that Jesus was taken to the high priest's house, but there is no account of the hearing itself before the high priest). John is no exception. In that Gospel Jesus undergoes an examination at the hands of both Caiaphas, the high priest, and Annas, the former high priest and father-in-law of Caiaphas. This is to suggest only one variation the Fourth Gospel has in the passion story while sharing the basic structure of the account with the Synoptics.

Second, you will notice that even with the deviation in chronology and order of events, the Fourth Gospel still has a basic structural similarity with the order of the ministry of Jesus recorded in the Gospel of Mark. We believe that the markan order was the foundation upon which the other two Synoptics were built, and some would propose that the Fourth Gospel is likewise dependent upon the markan order. The fourth evangelist follows this basic pattern which parallels the markan order.

1. The preaching of John the Baptist (Mark 1:4-8 and John 1:19-36)
2. The movement into Galilee (Mark 1:14f. and John 4:3)
3. The feeding of the crowd (Mark 6:34-44 and John 6:1-13)
4. Walking on the water (Mark 6:45-52 and John 6:16-21)
5. Peter's confession (Mark 8:29 and John 6:68f.)
6. Departure for Jerusalem (Mark 9:30f. and 10:1, 32, and 46 and John 7:10-14)
7. The entry into Jerusalem and the anointing (Mark 11:10 and 14:3-9 and John 12:12-15 and 1-8) (Notice John reverses the order of these two.)
8. A last supper (Mark 14:17-26 and John 13:1-17:26)
9. The passion story (Mark 14:43-16:8 and John 18:1-20:29)

(I have summarized the list of parallels offered by C.K. Barrett in his commentary on John.) The parallel is obvious even given the differences which we have already noted.

From this point on the similarities are less imposing upon the reader, but discernible nonetheless. Compare, for instance, the stories of the healing of the centurion's son in Matthew 8:5-13, the healing of the Syrophoenician woman in Mark 7:24-30, and the healing of the nobleman's son in John 4:46-54. There are some striking similarities even though the stories have different characters. There is a common portrayal of John the Baptist in the Synoptics and the Fourth Gospel: All identify him in much the same way and all have him predicting the appearance of the messiah.

Finally, one might not expect to find parallels between the speeches of Jesus in the Fourth Gospel and the Synoptics, but such parallels are there. You are invited to compare the following as examples:

John	Synoptics
"The man who loves himself is lost, but he who hates himself in this world will be kept safe for eternal life."(12:25)	"By gaining his life a man will lose it; by losing his life for my sake, he will gain it." (Matthew 10:39)
"In very truth I tell you, he who receives any messenger of mine receives me; receiving me, he receives the One who sent me." (13:20)	"To receive you is to receive me, and to receive me is to receive the One who sent me." (Matthew 10:40)
[To a paralytic Jesus says] "Rise to your feet, take up your bed and walk." (5:9)	[To a paralytic Jesus says] "I say to you, stand up, take your bed, and go home." (Mark 2:11)

There are also some comparable metaphors used by Jesus—e.g., the grain of wheat (John 12:24 and Matthew 5:13 or Mark 3:24). There are even dialogues which follow a pattern similar to those in a synoptic Gospel—e.g. John 7:3ff. and Luke 13:31ff. (For further similarities see C.H. Dodd, *Historical Tradition in the Fourth Gospel.)*

These similarities will have to suffice to convince you that there are striking parallels between the Fourth Gospel and the Synoptics. Sometimes that parallel is exclusively with one of the Synoptics, and sometimes it is with a common synoptic pattern. We must conclude, then, that the difference between the Synoptics and the Fourth Gospel emphasized above should be tempered with these similarities. Ah, but that is just the problem! The Fourth Gospel could more easily be explained if we had one without the other—that is, either its totally different account of the ministry of Jesus or its fully harmonious account. The way it is, with both differences and similarities, we have a far greater problem.

How shall we explain both these similarities and these differences at once? I propose that there are really three ways of accounting for the relationship of the maverick Gospel to its canonical colleagues: First, it has been argued that the fourth evangelist knew at least one or perhaps all of the synoptic Gospels and was to some degree dependent on it or them. He intended to write a "supplementary" Gospel by this theory. He assumed that the readers had some acquaintance with the synoptic account of Jesus and wanted to write a meditation, as it were, on that account. By this proposal, the evangelist was trying to write a "theological" or "spiritual" Gospel which would emphasize new aspects implicit in the synoptic Gospels. This view held sway for a number of years and is still advocated in some circles.

The opposite of this first proposal is that the fourth evangelist did not know the synoptic Gospels at all. He was writing to some degree out of his own knowledge and recollections without the assistance of the witnesses of the first three evangelists. The differences are obviously explained by this second theory, but the similarities are a bit more problematic. At the points of parallels with the synoptic Gospels, our second theory would propose, the fourth evangelist is simply reporting his memories which happen to be in accord with the synoptic witnesses.

The third view is the one with which I find myself in agreement. The fourth evangelist had access to a tradition which was associated with the synoptic traditions. That is, the dynamic oral transmission of the words and activities of Jesus took several different forms. One form of that tradition reached our evangelist. It was, by the time it came into his hands, quite distinctive from that which was incorporated into the synoptic Gospels, but it still showed evidence of having been spawned in the same pool of oral transmission with the synoptic materials. Diagrammatically, this view might by simplified as follows:

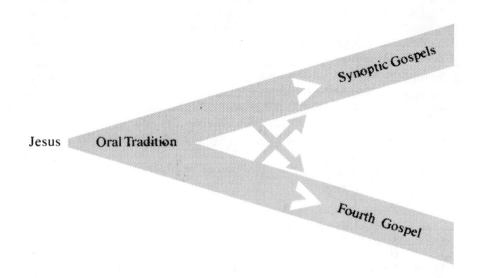

The oral tradition arising after the crucifixion of Jesus was an ever-expanding and growing body of sayings and narratives. This resulted from the church's effort to understand and relate to itself the ministry of the historical Jesus. But it was also the result of the faith that Jesus was still alive and active in the church, speaking through Christian prophets and teachers. Hence, the reservoir of "Jesus material" was not fixed by the simple memories of the eye-witnesses to his ministry, but was dynamic and growing. For whatever reason, it appears that two primary segments of that tradition developed. The one is known to us today by virtue of the synoptic Gospels, and the other is incorporated at least in part in the Fourth Gospel. (We could speak of still a third tradition which is represented in the letters of Paul.) Perhaps it was geography that accounts for the separation of the traditions; perhaps it was due to the peculiar interests and character of that community out of which the Fourth Gospel arose. The two streams of tradition were not entirely independent of one another. In addition to having a common source, there was interchange between them (suggested by the arrows intersecting between the two bodies of tradition). The result was that the two traditions were quite distinctive from one another, yet had some parallels and similarities.

The tradition reached our evangelist in a number of forms. There may have been some written materials which the evangelist incorporated into his Gospel. More than likely this included a document concerned primarily with the signs of Jesus, and included narratives of the seven wondrous signs of Jesus. In addition there were perhaps some other written materials passed on into the community of which the fourth evangelist was a member.

Surely, however, the oral tradition was still very rich and active when our evangelist worked. This means that much of what he heard in the life of his Christian community was not yet written down, but was handed on by word of mouth for the benefit of the Christian disciple.

With the benefit of this rich tradition, our evangelist—we will call him John for convenience—set about to write his Gospel. He wanted at once to be faithful to the traditional materials he knew and to be relevant to the community he addressed in his document. He was not unlike a good Christian theologian (or preacher) of our own day who tries faithfully to articulate the heritage of his or her religion in response to the burning questions of the day.

B. THE PURPOSE, DESTINATION, HISTORICAL ENVIRONMENT AND DATE OF
  THE FOURTH GOSPEL.

> *Reader's Preparation:* The following are important passages in the Gospel relevant to the questions with which we are dealing: (1) 20:30-31. (2) Chapter 9. (3) 6:22-58.

If the fourth evangelist intended to present his readers with a written expression of a tradition and to present it with as much relevance as possible, the question naturally arises, what was his specific *purpose* in doing so? What was he trying to accomplish? And precisely whom was he addressing? There are two levels on which we should proceed to deal with this question. First, does the writer make an explicit statement of purpose anywhere in the Gospel? Second, do other passages imply a purpose and destination which might not be explicitly stated?

John 20:30-31 would seem to be a clear indication of the purpose of the Gospel. What is written in the Gospel is intended to evoke faith on the part of the readers. To convince his readers that this Jesus is the messiah of Jewish expectation (the Christ) and a uniquely divine revealer (Son of God) is what it is all about. According to the reading of these verses, the evangelist hoped to win new believers to the faith. He hoped that his Gospel would be used as a missionary document to inspire belief among those who did not yet embrace the faith. The fourth evangelist was, then, an *evangelist* in the modern sense of the word—one who proclaims the Christian faith in order to win converts to the faith.

But this explicit statement of purpose for the Gospel is less than adequate in several ways. First of all, when we examine the Gospel as a whole it does not strike us as primarily a missionary document. Oh, to be sure, there are parts of it which read as if that was the purpose for which they were written. The prime example of such passages are the so-called signs of Jesus, for they appear to be told to evoke faith, just as 20:30-31 suggests. But much of the rest of the Gospel leaves the impression of having another purpose in mind. The discourses of Jesus, for instance, seem too complicated and sophisticated to have been intended for the non-believer. To speak analogically for a moment, the signs are the kind of thing a Billy Graham might write for his evangelistic purposes; but the discourses are for the most part more like something a theologian—let's say Paul Tillich—might write for the purposes of communicating an understanding of the faith to other believers.

Second, the explicit purpose cited in 20:30-31 seems to have been part of that tradition the evangelist is using. It is proposed, and I agree, that these verses once constituted the conclusion of the collection of signs material which the evangelist used. That source, let us suppose, was a missionary document comprised of the recounting of seven of Jesus' marvelous works. Verses 20:30-31 stood at the conclusion of the little book as a clear and accurate statement of its purpose. The fourth evangelist, having used the signs from this source, now appends its own conclusion to the end of his work in faithful recognition of his dependence upon the source. But it really is less appropriate for the Gospel than it was in its original setting. (Robert T. Fortna in *The Gospel of Signs* defends this view.)

The second place we look for the purpose of the Gospel is in the implications of the whole document. If you will grant me for the moment that the missionary goal is not entirely adequate as a proposed purpose of the Gospel, we will see what other suggestions we can find in the rest of the Gospel. There is one which is implied in a number of points but most clearly in the story of the healing of the blind man in chapter 9. What is suggestive about this story is not the healing itself, but what follows. The healing itself seems to fit that evangelistic purpose we have been considering. The account of the reaction of the authorities to the witness of the man who has just been healed is fascinating. After he has testified a second time to the fact that Jesus healed him and that Jesus must be from God, the authorities "expelled him from the synagogue." (v. 34). Then he encounters Jesus again and makes a full confession of faith (vv. 35-38). In the midst of this narrative we are told that the man's parents are fearful "for the Jewish authorities had already agreed that anyone who acknowledged Jesus as Messiah should be banned from the synagogue"(v. 22).

This account might suggest the kind of situation in which the evangelist found himself and one aspect of the reason for his writing the document. We know that some of the Jews who were converted to Christianity were formally banned from the synagogue late in the first century (the Council of Jamnia, ca. A.D. 90). What the story in chapter 9 seems to imply is that there was indeed a struggle going on between the Jews who did believe Jesus was the Messiah and those who did not. Some Jewish Christians were continuing to worship in the synagogue in the conviction that their new faith was not incompatible with their Jewish life and practice. The synagogue leaders in some locales, however, were not willing to accept this position and were seeking out and expelling from the Jewish worshipping community anyone who adhered to the Christian faith. In other words, there was an increasing tension between the Christians and the Jews *in the city in which John wrote.* That tension was mounting. Moreover, it was causing a good many persons a great deal of agony. Jews were being forced to surrender their Jewish roots, if they were adherents to the new faith. Christian leaders were caught in a dialogue with Jewish leaders.

I propose that something like this situation gives us a good insight into the situation and purpose of the evangelist. If this is the case, then a lot of things about the Gospel of John begin to make a great deal of sense. Let me only suggest a few. It is for this reason that the Gospel of John speaks as it does of "the Jews." It is not an ethnic category in the Fourth Gospel, but it is an allusion to the primary opponents of the johannine church at the time. For this reason to some degree the Gospel seems to play Jesus and Moses off against one another, or at least seems concerned to show that Jesus is superior to Moses (e.g., 1:16-17 and 6:32). The constant concern to describe Jesus as one sent from God and one who has divine status but still sub-ordinate to the Father is also elucidated. Could this not be the evangelist's response to charges from the Jewish leaders that Christians believe in two gods—Jesus and the Father? Perhaps, too, the dominance of the death plot against Jesus in the Fourth Gospel is explained. (That plot appears early in the Fourth Gospel, you will recall—5:18 and by implication back in 2:23-25—as opposed to the synoptic Gospels.) Perhaps the actual physical persecution of Christians by the Jews was giving new meaning to the suffering of Jesus at the hands of his fellow countrymen several decades earlier. Finally, Nicodemus (chapter 3) might be an example of what some Jews were doing in the evangelist's own day. They were secretly Christian or were secretly exploring the possibilities of Christian belief. But they did it under the cover of darkness, lest their colleagues discover their intent. (This proposal is founded upon the study of J. Louis Martyn, *History and Theology in the Fourth Gospel.*)

I think that as we explore the thought and symbolism of the Gospel of John further, it will become more and more obvious that this proposed situation for the writing of the Gospel makes a good deal of sense. The evangelist served a community locked in a crucial dialogue with the local Jewish synagogue. The Jewish opposition was threatening the Christian community, just as the Christian evangelistic efforts among the Jews were threatening the stability of the Jewish synagogue. The result was that both communities were defending themselves. The evangelist contributed to the defense of his community by addressing his writing primarily to members of that community. By using the traditions at his disposal and adapting them, he addressed a relevent message to his fellow Christians. He showed them how they might argue with their Jewish neighbors in response to the charges they posed against Christianity. He dramatically portrayed Jesus as himself engaged in a struggle with his fellow Jews who would not accept him and eventually put him to death. He showed them how Jesus was the comple-tion of the Mosaic tradition, not its contradiction. This was particularly relevant, for some of his readers (although not all) were of a Jewish heritage.

The primary purpose of the Gospel, then, was not evangelical, not missionary. It was addressed to the Christian community by one of their esteemed leaders. It was designed to strengthen them in their struggle in that local situation. It was, if you will, an intra-church document. It was a Gospel intended for the family. To be sure, the evangelist may have had hopes that some of the Jews who had some interest in the Christian faith would be persuaded by his writing. For that reason the missionary intent of 20:30-31 is not inappropriate. But the evangelist wanted less to convert than to nurture, less to evangelize than to encourage those already in the faith.

It may be a slight digression to do so, but it is important that we raise a question at this point in our discussion: Why did the evangelist choose to write a *gospel*? That is, in order to accomplish his purpose, why did the author select from among the many literary genre at his disposal this rather uniquely Christian form of literature we have come to call gospel? Of course, the author no where in his work calls it a gospel (unlike Mark 1:1). Still, he elects to give expression to his purpose by describing the figure of Jesus in something that at least appears to be a historical sequence. He might have written a pastoral letter (like Paul and others had done). He might have written a lengthy sermon and circulated it (in the manner of the author of Hebrews). Or he might have chosen an apocalypse as the form of his encouragement to fellow Christians in crisis (as did John of Patmos some years later).

This question is complicated, I believe, by the fact that the fourth evangelist did not know the other Gospels in their literary form. That is, he knew traditions (oral and written) which were ingredients for the gospel form, but had never seen a Christian gospel in its literary form. We believe that it was Mark who invented the gospel form out of Christian tradition (and perhaps with the knowledge of certain hellenistic literature which might have been similar to gospels). But if John had never seen the Gospel of Mark or one of the two other Gospels, how is it he came up with a Gospel of his own? Some would say that this question puts the lie to our contention that the fourth evangelist was not dependent upon the literary form of at least one of the synoptic Gospels. But I think there are other possibilities.

First, it has been proposed by some that the signs source which we believe the fourth evangelist used in writing his document was itself an early form of gospel genre. That is, it recounted the wondrous works of Jesus along with some other narrative materials in a historical sequence. And it did so with the purpose of proclaiming the faith. (That is, of course, the literal meaning of gospel—the proclamation of the "good news" of the faith.) John simply adopted that literary form from his source and filled it out with discourses and additional narratives (including perhaps the passion story). (See the works of Robert T. Fortna.)

A second possibility which strikes me as a bit more likely is that the oral tradition which the evangelist knew and used was already shaped in what we would call gospel form. Hence, in his attempt to re-present that tradition as faithfully as he could, he fell into the literary form of the gospel. This is to suggest that the creation of the literary gospel form is not so much the genius of the author of the written material (Mark and John), but it is the gradual and less than deliberate effort of the early Christian community to preserve the materials it had at its disposal. The oral tradition, then, based upon a historical recollection of Jesus of Nazareth, shaped itself into gospel. By filling out the historical material with legend, myth, and new teachings from what they believed to be the living Christ, the early Christians gradually shaped the gospel form in their pre-literary tradition.

But to return from our digression: This discussion has thus far laid out my point-of-view with regard to the purpose of the Gospel and the concrete situation which evoked its being written. Likewise, we have made clear that the Gospel was directed toward a community of Christians to which the evangelist probably belonged. It was a community comprised, I think, of Christians of a mixed background. Some were out of the Jewish tradition, as we have already seen. But others were doubtless of a gentile background. It is for that reason that the evangelist cannot assume that his reader understands Hebrew. Consequently, for instance, he is careful to translate certain Hebrew words—1:38 and 42. We are left now with one additional question—the intellectual environment of the evangelist.

If you want to understand a person, it is necessary to know a little about his or her background. If you want to understand your friend's strange reaction, say, to persons of the opposite sex, you may want to learn something about his or her parents and siblings. Only then can you understand why the person behaves as she or he does.

The same is true of a piece of literature. It helps to know a little bit about Shakespeare when you read his plays. The life of Albert Camus and the influence of French existentialism makes reading his novels significantly more enlightening.

We have tried to fill in some of that essential background for the Gospel of John, but we are left with the question of the intellectual influence upon his thought. What kinds of ideas had he come in contact with? What had he read that shaped his thought? Where did he borrow some of his expressions? All these are ways of asking about the intellectual atmosphere in which he worked—the conceptual air he breathed.

The situation in which the evangelist wrote already suggests the essential thing which we need to know for our purposes. First of all, it is obvious from what has been said above that I believe the evangelist was significantly influenced by Jewish thought. This means that the Jewish scriptures (the Old Testament) and extra-biblical writings were part of his intellectual diet.

There is evidence, however, that the Judaism which the fourth evangelist knew, and may have embraced at one time, was not simply the rabbinic Judaism which became the mainstream tradition after the first century. The parallels between johannine thought and the literature discovered in the so-called Dead Sea Scrolls are enough to convince us that the evangelist was acquainted with a broad type of Judaism which embraced a great variety of forms and expressions. We may find strikingly rabbinic-like features in the Gospel. For instance, the discourse in chapter 6 reads much like a rabbinic interpretation of a Scripture passage. But we also find many less than mainline rabbinic characteristics—the dualistic thought of his Gospel (see chapter two).

I cannot argue this position at length here. I only ask that you accept this as a tentative hypothesis upon which we can continue: The evangelist was primarily under the influence of a mixed Judaism. It was a Judaism which could tolerate a strict Pharisee on the one hand and an apocalyptic fanatic (like some of those responsible for the Dead Sea Scrolls) on the other. It was a Judaism which even tolerated for a time the Christian movement (as a sect) within its midst.

Such a Judaism as is described here, however, would not be free from influences coming upon it from the hellenistic world. Revived Greek philosophies. Mystery religions imported, in part, from the east. Speculative philosophies. Maybe even the Roman emperor cult. All these forms of religious and quasi-religious beliefs touched Judaism in the first century and the two previous centuries. The result was that the Judaism which influenced the fourth evangelist was no more pure of hellenistic thought than a democrat today is pure of all republicanism!

The consequence of this mixture of ideas and influences is that the fourth evangelist's conceptual storehouse was full to overflowing. He had at his disposal ideas fairly glistening with implications from different traditions. A ready example is the rich concept he employs to introduce his gospel, namely, the Word or (to use the Greek) *Logos*. Logos was a word which had profound roots in Greek philosophy—Stoicism, to be specific. But it was also founded on the Old Testament concept of the Word of God and was fleshed out with the Jewish speculation concerning Wisdom. We can imagine, then, that our evangelist often employed symbolism and ideas which were the product of the influence of numerous religious and philosophical heritages. He may have been conscious of the richness of many of these. But we can also imagine that some of his ideas and expressions may have been so commonplace to him that their richness was taken for granted. However that may be, the result was an evangelist peculiarly equipped to write a gospel of exciting concepts and puzzling breadth. It is just this, in part, which contributed to the formation of his maverick piece of early Christian literature.

There you have it: A man richly endowed with conceptuality and symbolism, the benefactor of a valuable and stimulating tradition, placed in a situation of crisis proportions for the Christian community. But when is it most likely that this took place? It is difficult to say with any certainty, and in a sense it is not necessary to decide a date for the Gospel with any precision. We know that the Fourth Gospel was circulating in Egypt before the middle of the first century, for the oldest fragment of New Testament material we have is a little chunk of the Gospel of John. That means, the scholars claim, that the Gospel had to have been written before the turn of the century.

We may assume, too, that it was not written before A.D. 70 when the Jerusalem Temple was destroyed in the war between the Jews and the Romans. The manner in which the Temple is alluded to in the Gospel has convinced most scholars of that.

We propose then a date of 80-90. The official expulsion of the Christians from the synagogue did not come until 90 A.D. But we think that such an official act could only have occurred in Judaism after it had become common practice in local synagogues throughout the hellenistic world. Therefore the date of 80-90 seems close enough for our purposes.

Perhaps you have wondered why we have come this far without any mention of the identity of the fourth evangelist who has come to be known as John. The reason for the delay is that I believe we can say almost nothing about him other than what has already been suggested in this chapter. He is and will probably remain forever anonymous to us. I do not believe that we can identify him with John, the son of Zebedee, one of the disciples of Jesus. Nor do I think that we are entitled to identify him with the mysterious "disciple whom Jesus loved" in the Fourth Gospel. We have described some of his background which qualified him for his task of writing this Gospel. Moreover, we have claimed that the tradition available to him was rich and full. To venture more than this about the writer would be to venture too far out on the limb of speculation. We will continue to call him the fourth evangelist and even "John," but I think we must settle for his anonymity.

What we have attempted to do in this introductory chapter is suggest the manner in which the Fourth Gospel is the maverick of the canonical gospels—that it "walks on its hands" as compared with the Synoptics. Moreover, it has been proposed that there are reasons for this Gospel's maverick nature. It was written on the basis of a tradition that was distinct from that embodied in the Synoptics. It was written by an evangelist who was uniquely equipped with a vast array of concepts and symbolism arising out of a mixed Judaism and influenced by hellenistic thought as well. It was addressed to the Christian church amid a vital struggle with the Jewish synagogue—a situation which called for new and radical ideas. All of these contributed to the final product: A gospel which did not easily conform to the developing "standard bland" of Christianity. We can be grateful to the early church for not excluding the Fourth Gospel from its canon. Had they done so, we would be far poorer.

It is now time to turn to the exposition of the religious thought and symbolism of this Gospel. That exposition will further demonstrate the point made in this chapter, I think, namely, that the Fourth Gospel is a different sort of early Christian thought. At the same time, we will begin to see how universal the Fourth Gospel is in its thinking and how it supplies us with a prime example of the way religious persons wrestle with a series of vital questions.

1. The Father's Son—Johannine Christology

THE HISTORY OF RELIGIONS is filled with accounts of extraordinary founders of religious movements. Most (but not all) of the major religious traditions of the world are rooted in some one originator. These traditions look back to that founder in recognition of his or her role in uncovering the gem of truth which has become characteristic of the religion. These founding figures are claimed to have had some sort of special revelation or inspiration. That insight has been preserved through the institutional structures of the religion for later generations. The founder of the tradition, at least, is the historical origin of the faith.

Likewise, every religious tradition rooted in a historical figure develops claims for the uniqueness of the founder's person as well as his or her revelation. This development is elaborate and varied. In some cases, the experience of the founder is the type of religious experience available to all of the devout followers of the faith. Such would appear to be the case in some forms of Buddhism, for instance, where the enlightenment of Guatama is the goal of all those who adhere to the religion. In other cases, the uniqueness of the founder is so stressed that it is not her or his experience which can be repeated, but an experience *of the founder*. Traditional Christianity would seem to be an example of this view. But in either case, the uniqueness of the founder and his or her revelation is vital to the development of the religion. That uniqueness tends to be viewed as a self-evident fact about the historical figure of the founder. So, Mohammed, Moses, Zoroaster, Guatama are believed by their respective religions to have been certain and conspicuous in their extraordinary qualities.

The claim for the uniqueness of the founder is, however, a development in these traditions. That is, the religion elaborates on the nature of their founder until eventually something like a final and "orthodox" view emerges. The final view may range all the way from a simple claim for peculiar piety (Mohammed), to extraordinary birth (Gautama), to divine nature (Christ). What is obviously similar among the world religions is that nearly all have a founder for whom they make radical claims and that those claims have developed within the history of the religion. The truth of the claim is usually hidden in the obscurity of history, but it is clearly witnessed to by the adherents of the faith.

It is the struggle of a religious tradition to define the nature of its founder that interests us at this point. The explication of the nature of the founder is one of the early and vitally important stages in the emergence of a major religious tradition. Take up the study of almost any religion, and you will find a fascinating history of the maturation of views of its founder. In the Jewish tradition, for instance, one finds already in the Old Testament itself a honorific attitude toward Moses (e.g., Deuteronomy 34:10). Then in Jewish thought following the close of the Old Testament period there is elaborate speculation about Moses. Legends abound. It is asserted, for instance, that Moses never really died but was taken up into heaven *(The Assumption of Moses)*. A religious tradition does not easily come upon its definition of its founder. That is the result of a long process of thought and discussion, of formulation and reformulation.

The truth of these remarks for early Christianity is clear. The struggle of Christians to settle upon some common view of the nature of Jesus of Nazareth begins in the earliest years of the movement. It climaxes (but does not end) in the Nicene Council and its creedal statement (325). The New Testament presents us with ample evidence of the efforts of the early Christians to formulate what they wanted to say about Jesus, his person and his work. If one tries to abstract from the New Testament a single, consistent view of Christ, trouble arises. It seems to say a number of different things about the person of Jesus. The picture one gets, I think, is of early Christian thinkers struggling to find words adequate to express their faith about Christ.

The Fourth Gospel represents an important contribution to that emerging view of Christ among the first century Christians. It takes up the Christ figure with a different point-of-view and makes some radical statements on the question. It is fair to say that with the Fourth Gospel the view of Christ in early Christian thinking made a giant leap forward in one direction. As it happened, that direction proved eventually to be the way the later church would go in its statements of faith about the person of Christ. Still, we should not approach the Fourth Gospel with the impression that it has one consistent view of Christ which it intends to propagate. The Gospel, too, presents not one but a number of assertions about the religion's founder. Those statements are not always fully consistent with one another in the way that a modern theologian would like them to be. But they tend to move in a singular direction. The importance of those assertions for later Christian thought is hard to overemphasize.

This chapter will look at a number of aspects of the Fourth Gospel in terms of what they claim for the person and work of Christ. Four topics will occupy us for the remainder of this chapter: (1) The Logos or Word christology of the prologue of the Gospel. (2) The variety of titles for Christ employed in 1:19-51. (3) The Son of Man and the relationship of the Father and Son in the Gospel. (4) The importance of the "I am" sayings for christology.

A. THE LOGOS CHRISTOLOGY

Reader's Preparation: Read again the prologue of the Gospel (1:1-18). Pay special attention to what it affirms concerning the nature and work of the Word.

These first eighteen verses of the Fourth Gospel are among the most significant of the entire New Testament. They are also among the most puzzling. It is accurate to say that this passage is one of the most frequently studied portions of early Christian literature. There are a number of concerns about this passage which we are going to ignore, and I think the reader ought to be alerted to them. The first is the hymnic quality of these verses. Many students of the Fourth Gospel sense that the bulk of the passage reads like a piece of poetry, and they speculate that it was used in Christian worship in some way or another. This presents a further question: Did the fourth evangelist write these words, or did he incorporate a popular Christian hymn at the first of his Gospel? (The latter might have been a good attention "grabber" with which to begin his work.) Or, is it possible that these verses were attached to the Gospel some time after it had been written? The proposal that it is a later addition has one strong piece of evidence in its favor: Nowhere else in the Gospel is the Word referred to in any way similar to its use in these verses. If the evangelist had composed this passage, or even if he had used a Christian hymn as the introduction to his Gospel, would it not be likely that he would have explicitly tied the rest of his work in with the affirmation of this introduction?

I am going to assume that the affirmations of this passage have some themes consistent with the christology of the rest of the Gospel. Hence, I will treat it as an integral part of the affirmations about Christ in the Gospel. But by doing so I do not want to suggest that the prologue is unquestionably a part of the work of the evangelist. As a matter of fact, it is my opinion that the prologue more than likely was a late addition to the Gospel. Perhaps it was attached to the Gospel by the evangelist himself after he had finished his work. Perhaps it was appended by a later reviser of the Gospel. One way or another, it is there, and we must study it for what it says about the view of Christ held either by the evangelist or by the community that preceded or followed him.

The introductory chapter has already alluded to the richness of the idea of the Word or the Logos. Much time is spent in seeking out the historical precedents of this concept. Our concern is only to expand the point we have already made. That point is that the Logos was an idea which had roots in several different religious and philosophical settings. First, in stoicism current in hellenistic philosophies, the Logos was conceived as a sort of cosmic reason. It was the mind at the center of the universe. It gave order and structure to the whole sense of the operation of the universe. A bit of that universal Logos resides in every person, this view affirmed, and hence related every person to the heart of the cosmos.

But, of course, the Hebrews had an equally ancient tradition of the Word of God—the *dahbar Yahweh*. It was the Word of God which brought all existence into being, according to the tradition embedded in Genesis 1. It was the Word of God which addressed the prophets and filled them with their message for the Hebrew people. It is as if the Word of God was the bridge between the transcendent God of Hebraic thought and the human world.

Later Jewish thought made much of the concept of wisdom. Wisdom resided with God and informed the devout person. Wisdom is made into a divine being, in a sense, in some Jewish literature like Proverbs 8:22-31. Late in the Old Testament period and beyond that period through the first century of the Christian era, Jewish speculation about wisdom related it to the Torah, the written word of God. Likewise, it became identified with the Word of God (*memra*, the Aramaic for "word"). So, in an oversimplified way of summarizing a long history, wisdom was personified then tied in and harmonized with the earlier tradition of the Word of God.

It is out of this rich heritage that the author of the prologue of the Gospel drew his meaning. One can see how the meaning of the prologue could be similar to the significance of the Logos in Stoic thought, how it relates to the Old Testament concept of Word of God, and how it is almost a translation (wisdom to word) of the wisdom speculation of Jewish thought. Whatever its specific roots, the author intends it, I think, to have a rich and varied meaning. He may have wanted its specific precedents to be allusive so that both his Jewish and his gentile readers could resonate with its meaning.

But further our author intends to say something specific about Jesus with these concepts. He intends to apply this broad religious-philosophical category of Logos to Jesus in order to say that Jesus fulfilled the whole vast tradition of many different religions and philosophical views of the universe. The author is saying, in effect: Yes, Christ is all of this—Stoic Logos, Old Testament Word, and Jewish Wisdom—rolled into one person. And that is the thrust of the prologue, I believe: Logos for the Christian is a *person*. The Logos is not an abstract philosophical concept. It is not a category of religious experience. Nor is it speculative religious mythology. It is person, infreshed, living, historical person. Therein lies the genius of the prologue. It claims the abstract, the subjectively experienced, the myth has become and is person. That is quite a claim. Whether you believe it is true or not, you must recognize its importance as a Christian claim for Christ.

But let's get into the prologue itself. What does the passage affirm about this Logos? The following is said about the Word:

Existed from the beginning
  Existed with God
    Was God
      Was the agent of creation
        Was life which was light to persons
          (Was not John the Baptist)
            Was in, but not recognized by, the world
            Was rejected by his own
              Was source of power to become children of God
                Became flesh and dwelt in the world
              Revealed Glory
            Was God's Son
          (John the Baptist witnessed to him)
        Was the means of grace and truth
      Was superior to Moses
    Made God known as never before

A number of these affirmations demand our examination, not least of which is the very first. This constitutes one of the highest claims the Christian has made for Christ: He existed from the beginning. The pre-existence of the Logos affirms not only that he existed before creation itself, but that he existed before "all things began." His existence goes back into that mysterious time before time—into the realm of temporality which eludes human conceptuality. While we cannot fathom what it would mean to exist before all else, we can try to fathom what the author is trying to affirm by saying this. Christ is so important that he could not simply have come into being like any other person or object. Christ is made to transcend beings and things by the assertion of his pre-temporal existence. The evangelists responsible for the Gospels of Matthew and Luke said something like this when they incorporated the myths of the virgin birth and/or conception by the Holy Spirit. They were affirming that Christ's significance in the lives of persons precludes his having come into being in an ordinary way. His origin is by extraordinary divine initiative. The fourth evangelist (or the author of the prologue) has gone one step further to say the same thing. Christ is no created being. He is before creation. The point I want to stress is that this affirmation is an expression of the sense of the absolute significance of Christ.

Another affirmation which leaps out from among those in the prologue is that the Logos was the agent of creation. "Through him all things came to be; no single thing was created without him." (v. 3) There is here a fascinating expansion of Christian thought about Christ. The earliest Christians surely affirmed the redeeming quality of the life and death of Jesus of Nazareth. He is the source of a new kind of life—one arruned with the divine purpose for human existence. But somewhere in the growth of early Christian thought came a further step—a leap, I would say. This redeeming, saving person is also the agent of divine creation. He is not only an agent of redemption but of creation as well. Our prologue may or may not have been the first known literary expression of that idea. It vies for the honor with the christological hymn in Colossians 1:15-20 (see especially v. 16). But what an overwhelming idea it is! Again one is driven to ask what the early Christians meant to say with this concept of Christ as the creative agent. They might well have neatly kept the function of Christ confined to divine redemption. But, no, they had to go further and complicate matters by assigning him a function in creation. Surely the affirmation again arises from roots in the existential meaning of Christ for human life. So fundamental to the sense and purpose of existence is the revelation in Christ that he must be conceived as the shaping force in the very beginnings of existence!

What then is the relationship of this pre-existent, creative Logos to God himself? The prologue is tantalizing at this point. It is almost as if the author is teasing his reader with the language of his first verse. The Greek reads something like this: "The Logos was with the God." The preposition "with" suggests relationship. "And the Word was God." God and the Word are identified. The definite article before "God" in the first clause of the sentence is missing in the second. That little grammatical detail has suggested to some that the identity of the Logos and God is not intended to be complete. It means something like, "The Logos was divine." I think, however, that such an interpretation is pressing the significance of the absence of the definite article too far.

This sentence of the prologue, I believe, introduces the reader immediately to a basic view of Christ in the Fourth Gospel: The Logos is a distinct being, yet identical with God. That is, there is both *individuality* and *identification* in the relationship between God and Logos (or Christ). "With God"—"Was God"! We do not want to make the prologue read like a later church christological confession. This is written at a time long before the church wrestled with trinitarian concepts. Still, honest interpretation of the passage necessitates that we understand the author to introduce us here to a paradox at the heart of the relationship of Christ and God. How can there be individuality (distinctiveness, separateness, twoness) and identity (oneness, sameness) at the same time? The author does not tell us. One can almost hear him laughing in the wings as we try to stretch our minds to get them around the meaning of his words.

At least, the author means that Christ is the expressive dimension of divine being. That is, that the Logos-Christ is God's revealing, outward directed activity. Let me invoke one of my simplistic analogies: A person may be said to have two sides or dimensions. There is that side of a person's being which expresses who she or he is. In actions and words to friends and intimates, one reveals who he or she is. But there is another side to personal being. It is that inner, unexpressed (or seldom expressed) dimension. Depending upon the quality of intimacy one has with others, this side of personal being may be sizable or nearly negligible. Forgive the application, but the Logos is that expressed, outward side of God. That does not mean that God is exhausted in the Logos, but (the Christians would affirm) the significance of divine existence for humans is manifested in that expressive being of God. If this is what the author of the prologue has in mind, he is saying that Logos is that dimension of God which has come to expression for the comprehension of humans.

This leads us to the heart of the prologue as it now stands in the Gospel—the famous verse 14: "So the Word became flesh; he came to dwell among us..." The expression of divine being takes up abode in a single human creature and lives among other humans for a time. The expressive side of God's being is *physically* present. It is made sensual to be touched, seen, heard, and felt. This "sensual Logos" is, of course, for the fourth evangelist the man, Jesus of Nazareth. This statement constitutes the normative affirmation of incarnational christology for Christianity. It has been claimed that the Logos is God and now Logos has become human person.

One cannot, I think, grasp the full significance of this effort to articulate the identity of the founder of the Christian movement without briefly comparing it to other such statements in the New Testament. It could be argued that there are three fundamental forms of the concepts of Christ in the New Testament. We will label them the "adoptionistic," the "agency," and the "incarnational."

The adoptionistic christology suggests that Jesus was a man who because of his obedience to God was adopted as God's Messiah. This adoption may have taken place sometime in the ministry of Jesus, but more often it is declared to have been the meaning of the resurrection. By this view there is no pre-existence of Christ or even divine initiative in his birth. He lives an obedient life and is then made God's special person, his Messiah. This kind of christological thought, I believe, was the earliest way by which Christians conceived of their founder. But it is only faintly present in the literature of the New Testament, for Christians very soon began thinking of Christ in (shall we say) more noble terms. The presence of an early adoptionistic christology, however, lurks behind these passages in the New Testament: Acts 2:36 and 3:13 and Romans 1:3-4. (For further defense of this position see J.A.T. Robinson, *Twelve New Testament Studies*, pp. 139-153.)

Agency christology is more common in the New Testament. In some form it declares that God took the initiative to send a personal agent to perform a revelatory and saving function. This kind of thinking is present in all those passages in the New Testament which are satisfied simply to say that Jesus was "sent" by God. Interestingly enough, it is one of the favorite expressions of the Fourth Gospel to say comething like this(e.g., 3:34). But it is also represented in other New Testament literature such as Matthew 10:40 and Romans 8:3. Jesus is thus sometimes conceived as a prophet of God sent out with a message and mission. But I take it that the birth narratives of Matthew and Luke are essentially expressions of a form of agency christology. In this case, the agent is more than just a man. His being is shaped by God's special action in one way or another. Still, whether the nature of the agent is that of a specially chosen person or an extra-human being, his function is to be an agent, a representative, or, if you will, a diplomat.

But the boldest of claims for Christ are embodied in the incarnational christologies. In this way of conceiving of Christ, some form of his prior existence is asserted. That is, he is thought to have existed before his appearance as a man in this world. This is equal in importance to and logically necessitated by the central theme of incarnational christology: The divine being has become a human person. The contribution of incarnational christology is then to claim the divine nature of Christ and at the same time to claim that the divine Christ has taken a human form. The prologue of the Fourth Gospel is the fullest and clearest statement of incarnational christology in the New Testament. But Colossians 1:15-20 nearly rivals the prologue for its incarnational affirmation. The Philippian hymn (2:6-11) is often debated, but it may express a similar view.

If I might, I would like to borrow and adapt from Reginald H. Fuller diagrammatic summaries of these three views. (See *The Foundations of New Testament Christology*, pp. 243-46.)

The prologue of the Fourth Gospel, then, presents us with the finest specimen of early Christian incarnational thought. Here most clearly is the divine nature of the pre-existent Logos affirmed and here is the humanization or infleshment of that Logos flatly declared. Not only does the fourteenth verse declare that humanization, but it suggests more. The verb

Adoptionistic:

God's
Adoption

Jesus' Life of Obedience

Christ's
Exaltation
to Messiah

Agency:

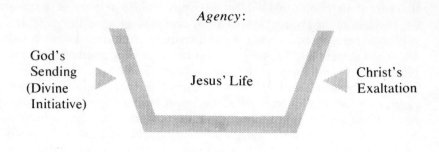

God's
Sending
(Divine
Initiative)

Jesus' Life

Christ's
Exaltation

Incarnational:

Christ's Pre-Earthly
Existence (Or, Existence
Before Creation)

Christ's Post-earthly
Existence

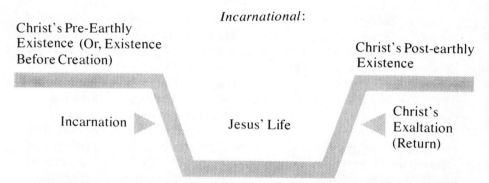

Incarnation

Jesus' Life

Christ's
Exaltation
(Return)

translated "dwell" literally means something like "put up camp for a while." The implication is that the Logos is upon a journey, and he camped out in this world for a time as a part of his itinerary. Here the heart of Christian gospel is articulated. It is not our task to argue for or against that gospel, but only to point out and to marvel at the religious mind (or community of minds) responsible for it.

I would call the content of the prologue prime Christ myth. I mean by that not that the claims for Christ made here are necessarily untrue. (Surely that misuse of the word "myth" is due to be put to rest once and for all.) I mean that these claims for the cosmic, extra-worldly existence and behavior of the Logos are poetic and imaginative in the most profound sense. They are means of expressing the significance and status of Christ in the personal lives of the Christian community. The prologue bursts out of mundane, historical, and "factual" description to tell us something about the early Christians and their perception of reality. The myth is that perspective upon human life and the world which informed and structured existence for them. Whenever one declares what it is that gives life meaning and purpose, he or she speaks mythologically. To do so is to throw up a model of understanding for the world which accurately fits the experience and stance of the believer. This is the function the Christ myth of the prologue played in the community out of which it arose. It articulated that model of meaning and purpose. It presented a cosmic perspective within which all of the experience of the worshipping community could by encompassed. It articulated a perspective within which life could be lived without deadly fear and/or utter despair. So it is that every religious community articulates itself in myth which gives meaning to life. Our prologue is a supreme example of such myth in the origins of Christianity.

B. THE CHRISTOLOGICAL TITLES IN 1:19-51

Reader's Preparation: Read 1:19-51. List all of the titles used in reference to Christ in the passage. Also note any other claims made for him there.

Chapter one of the Gospel proves to be packed to the brim with chris-tological affirmations. The prologue has confronted us with the claims associated with the Logos and his incarnation. But in the verses following the conclusion of the prologue there occurs a whole series of titles applied to Christ. Actually a survey of these titles is in effect a summary of many of the major labels by which the Fourth Gospel explicates its understanding of Christ.

The first title for Christ to confront the reader in this passage is found on the lips of John the Baptist: The Lamb of God (vv. 29 and 36). This title evokes a whole series of possible meanings which we will only sketch. Like most of the titles used of Christ here (and elsewhere in the New Testament, as far as that goes), this one could have a number of meanings. The most obvious is the one we have already mentioned in the Introduction, namely, the paschal lamb. The lamb had special affiliations with the Passover celebration and would evoke images of the liberation of the people from bondage. But the Baptist further qualifies the sense of the expression lamb of God by saying, "It is he who takes away the sin of the world." This suggests that the meaning of the expression is not the Passover lamb, but a sacrificial lamb. It is one whose death is symbolic of the remorse of the worshippers. Its death is expiatory in some way—that is, it is offered to God and its offering removes sin. The Passover lamb and the sacrificial lamb may have been associated, although the Passover lamb was not slain as a formal sacrifice.

The third association the title Lamb of God has is with the figure who appears in much Jewish apocalyptic literature. There is much of this literature which has a lamb in the drama of the end times. This lamb is a central figure in the destruction of evil in the world. It is this sort of lamb imagery which appears in Revelation (e.g., chapter 5). Finally, the suffering servant of 2 Isaiah (42:1-4; 49:1-6; 50:4-9; and 52:13–53:12) is described as a lamb in one of the passages (53:7). Since many believe that the early Christians interpreted Christ out of the context of this suffering servant imagery, it is natural that there are many who find servant allusions in this use of the title Lamb of God. (I am indebted to Raymond Brown's commentary on John for some of this summary of possible meanings in the title.)

What do we have then? The evangelist may mean to say about Christ by using the Lamb of God title any or all of these: (a) He is the symbol of the new Passover, the new liberation from bondage offered by God. (b) He is the innocent victim whose suffering and death has the effect of gaining the removal of human sin. (c) He is the figure who appears at the end of time to destroy all evil in the world. (d) He is the servant of God whose suffering atones for the sin of others. There is little of the apocalyptic notions of Christ as the destroyer of evil in the rest of the Gospel. As we will see, apocalyptic themes are not strongly represented in the Gospel. The Passover reference has much to say for itself, since (as we have seen) it is by the evangelist's scheme of things that Jesus is crucified precisely at the time the Passover lambs are being slain in preparation for the meal. That idea of liberation is surely associated with the sacrificial lamb—the victim whose death effects the release from sin. That idea, in turn, has clear roots in the concept of the suffering servant in 2 Isaiah.

What the evangelist wants us to understand, then, by the claim that Jesus is the Lamb of God is, I believe, that this is the agent of God whose life and death results in liberation. There is in the Fourth Gospel a minimum of language and thought which suggests that Jesus is conceived as an expiation for sin. The death of Jesus is not so much a sacrifice as an ironic means of exaltation of Jesus for our evangelist. Therefore, it is likely that the fourth evangelist wanted the liberating qualities of Christ to be understood in broader terms than that of an expiatory death. "You shall know the truth, and the truth will set you free" (8:32), and of course, it is Christ himself who is the truth, according to the Fourth Gospel (14:6). The Lamb of God is the liberating revealer of God. His freeing function occurs not strictly in his suffering and death, but in his very person. To know him is to be freed. In this way, the fourth evangelist has employed the title Lamb of God but given it a new and fresh meaning which is nonetheless not discontinuous with its previous meanings.

The second title we meet in this passage is the first of several which all have the same essential meaning, namely, Jesus' messiahship. "God's Chosen One" (v. 34), "Messiah" (v. 41), "The man spoken of by Moses in the Law, and by the prophets" (v. 45), and "king of Israel"(v. 49). They all are ways of referring to the special agent of God who is to come. They all are packed with Jewish expectation for an ideal king who will rule justly. But all the messianic titles were suggestive of more than a political ruler by the first century of the Christian era. They connoted one who would rescue the people from economic as well as political oppression; he would correct religious injustices and falsehoods. He would destroy the forces of evil in the world. He was variously thought of as a man, a superman, and an angelic type of divine creature.

What the evangelist is emphasizing in these titles is the conviction that this Jesus was indeed the fulfillment of the whole body of messianic expectations. Faced as he was with opposition from the Jewish leaders of his city, the fourth evangelist wants to make one fact clear at the very beginning of this Gospel: Jesus is the Messiah. And so the whole range of titles used of the Messiah are here grouped together to make that point. "Is there any one who is still unsure about whether or not we Christians believe Jesus to be the Messiah?" John has said it loud and clear. But he wants to say more. Jesus is all of this, but more.

That leads us to the title, "Son of God," used in verse 49. Here we have to ask again what historical precedents have converged to produce the meaning the evangelist intends. Son of God may mean from its Old Testament background simply the anointed king of Israel. Hence, it is the one especially chosen by God (e.g., 2 Samuel 7:14). The people of Israel themselves are sometimes called sons of God (Hosea 1:10). It is out of the hellenistic world that the concept of the Son of God as a divine being emerges. The divine man is one especially gifted with powers that have their source in deity. That title was adopted by the Christians very early as a title for Christ and was intended to convey his special status in relation to God (e.g., Romans 8:3).

To what extent does the evangelist intend to say that Christ is one of divine nature by having this title applied to him? We will explore the use of the general title Son below. There we will see he means it to carry a special weight of divinity. But here the title Son of God appears in close association with the messianic title. Nathanael is made to use the title Son of God as an apparent synonym for "King of Israel." Hence, here it has a traditional messianic sense, I believe. This is the meaning which the evangelist wants to explode into a greater meaning. He wants to show that Jesus is indeed the Messiah, the Son of God, the King of Israel, but he is much more than that.

Before we go to the climax of this series of christological titles in the second part of the first chapter, we must note another issue which is present in this passage. Along with these titles there is a persistent theme of the relationship of Jesus and John the Baptist. In the course of the narrative about the witness of the Baptist to Christ, three points are made with regard to the relationship of the Baptist and Christ:

a. Christ is greater than the Baptist. We are told this not once but twice. The Baptist is not good enough even to bend down and loosen Jesus' shoes (v. 27), for Christ ranks far ahead of the Baptist (v. 30).

b. The Baptist is made to say, "Before I was born, he already was." (v. 30). This might mean simply that Jesus is older than John. But given the theme of the pre-existence of Christ in the Gospel (8:58 as well as the prologue), it is pretty clear that the evangelist here has the Baptist witnessing to the pre-existence of Christ.

c. The Baptism of John is with water. Christ baptizes with the Holy Spirit
(v. 33). Clearly the assertion is made that Christ is superior to the
Baptist by virtue of Christ's bestowing the gift of the Spirit itself. John's
gift is a water baptism, symbolic of repentance.

We should add to this list the assertion of the prologue that John was not
the light but only a witness to the light (v. 8).

Why all this concern to show that Jesus is superior to John the Baptist? It
is argued by some that the fourth evangelist knew a group of persons who
believed that the Baptist was the Messiah. Hence, his argument here is
against those persons. This is possible, for it does seem that the Baptist
attracted around himself a group of followers. They very well might have
claimed their leader to be the Messiah, especially after his death. More
likely, I believe, is that here again the evangelist is answering a charge
leveled against Christians by Jewish leaders. The Jews were saying, "Your
Jesus was just another prophetic voice similar to that of the Baptist. He was
nothing more!" The evangelist is answering that charge with the claim that
Jesus is in an entirely different category than the Baptist. To make his reply
carry the greatest possible weight, he has put this point on the lips of John
the Baptist himself.

So, Jesus is all of these: Lamb of God, God's Chosen One, Messiah, the
man spoken of by Moses in the Law and by the prophets, King of Israel,
and far greater than John the Baptist. But now we reach the climax, I think,
of this little treatise on the identity of Jesus. The last title used of Christ in
this series is "Son of Man." It is important that the evangelist has Jesus
receive all of the previous titles. Jesus is never made to object or correct the
various confessions directed toward him. But after Nathanael's strong
confession in verse 49, Jesus replies: "You shall see heaven wide open, and
God's angels ascending and descending upon the Son of Man" (v. 51).
Surely Jesus is the Messiah in the sense that all of these titles suggest.
Surely he is greater than John the Baptist. But what he really is is tucked
away in the meaning of this expression, Son of Man.

Pages have been written in quest of the meaning of this title. It is enough
for us here to say simply that this title denoted a special divine agent of God.
Jewish mythology had given birth to a heavenly man figure who resided
with God from creation. He would come among humans at a time of God's
choosing, at the end of the present age. He would overcome evil and
establish the reign of God upon the earth. He represented the messianic
figure but also a figure whose nature was extra-human. He was at once the
prototype of human beings and the eschatological restorer of humanity. His
being is mysterious and hidden until that time when he is destined to enter
history and bring it to its grand climax. (See for example Daniel 7:13-14.)

I think the evangelist is saying, if you want to use a title for Christ, it is the
title Son of Man which best befits him. John seems clearly to prefer this title

among the various ones he employs for Jesus. This is so for a number of reasons: First, the Son of Man title had a prominent place in the tradition the evangelist received. Of course, the Fourth Gospel shares this title and its prominence with the synoptic Gospels. This is one of the points at which the traditions are in common. But, second, the evangelist may have preferred this title to the others because it gave him some elbow room. It was a mysterious being this title designated. Our evangelist liked that, for he could use that ambiguity to his advantage. He shaped the meaning of Son of Man out of the convictions which he, his tradition, and his community had about Christ. This title permitted him to develop his claims for Christ in a creative way, for it burst out of the pre-conceived notions of the Messiah.

Out of this title, Son of Man, I think the evangelist used his own favorite title, simply Son. It is that designation for Jesus which by far dominates the titles for Christ in the Fourth Gospel, and we have only scratched the surface of johannine christology until we have looked deeper into the affirmations of the Fourth Gospel about the Son in his relationship with the Father. (I am convinced that the Son title functions as an abbreviation of the Son of Man title, but you should be aware that some understand Son to be more closely related to the Son of God title. Others take the title, Son, as a special johannine synthesis of the meanings of both the Son of Man and Son of God titles.)

C. THE SON OF MAN AND THE FATHER-SON RELATIONSHIP

Reader's Preparation: In order to understand the heart of johannine christology, you should read the following scattered passages for what they say about the Son of Man and the relationship between the Father and Son:
1. The Son of Man passages: 1:51; 3:13-15; 5:27; 6:27; 6:53; 6:62; 8:28; 9:35-38; 12:23; 12:34-36; 13:31.
2. The Father-Son relationship: 3:16-17; 3:31-35; 4:34; 5:19-23; 5:37; 6:29; 6:38; 6:40-46; 7:16; 7:28-29; 8:16; 8:36-38; 8:42; 8:54; 10:17; 10:30-38; 12:45-49; 14:9-11; 14:20; 14:28; 16:5; 16:28; 17:8; 17:11-24.

The Son of Man title and its abbreviation, Son, constitute the heart of johannine christology. It is our task now to try to get into what the fourth evangelist says about the Son of Man and his relationship with the Father. We will try to do this through summarizing in a number of statements what the relevant passages seem to say. You are invited to test these assertions against the evidence you have been asked to examine in the Gospel.

First, Jesus is the Son of Man (9:35-38). This is an obvious point, perhaps, but needs to be asserted in the beginning. The evangelist wants his readers to understand that the man Jesus of Nazareth was indeed this mysterious Son of Man.

Second, his home is in the heavenly realm with God. 3:13-15 is the simplest statement of this idea. The Son of Man originates in that heavenly home, descends into the human world, and will once again ascend after the completion of his task (3:13; 6:62; 16:28). The emphasis here is that this figure does not belong to this world. His origin is elsewhere—it is divine. He appears mysteriously from nowhere, lingers among persons for a time, and then departs. Hence, there is a great deal of discussion in the Fourth Gospel about where Jesus is from. When he claims to be the bread which has come down from heaven, his opponents are puzzled. They say they know his father and mother. They know where he is from, and it isn't heaven (6:42-43)! Similarly, they cannot believe that the Messiah would be from Galilee (7:41). When Jesus speaks of his ascent once again to heaven, his hearers are further confused: Maybe he means he is going to kill himself (8:22)! The descent and ascent themes are good examples of the way in which the evangelist represents the crowd as totally misunderstanding the words of Jesus. The origin of the Messiah was an important credential for Jewish thought in the first century, and our evangelist uses that concern to make his point repeatedly that the Son of Man has no worldly origin.

Third, associated with his heavenly origin and destination is the idea that the Son has been *sent* by the Father. The passages which express this idea are too numerous to examine; suffice it for now to mention 3:34; 8:26; 4:34; 9:4; 17:3. Like a kind of cosmic prophet, the Son is sent forth into the world of humans. As one sent by God, he represents the Father and speaks for him. Typical of the emissary thought of the time, the one sent carries the authority of the sender. (We will note the authority of the Son of Man below.) Like a diplomatic envoy, the Son is commissioned by the Father, carries the authority of the Father, and acts in his behalf. Much of what we have to say below about the authority of the Son of Man and his assumption of the functions of the Father are rooted here in the concept of his being sent. What we have called the agency christology figures very prominently in the christology of the Fourth Gospel. But this agent is no mere prophet (like John the Baptist?). He is none other than the Son of Man.

The *fourth* assertion about the Son of Man is related to his ascent into heaven. The sayings relevant to this ascent are of two kinds. The first are those in which Jesus is made to speak of his "glorification." He claims that his death is his glorification (12:23) and that his glorification is the glorification of the Father (13:31). The irony is already obvious. He will die and his death will be in actual fact his glorification. But the second kind of passages intensify that irony. Jesus is made to speak again and again of his being "lifted up" (e.g., 3:13-15). The Greek word here is an ambiguous one. It can mean the act of crucifying—lifting the victim up onto the cross. But it can also mean exaltation—the honoring of a person. In having Jesus speak of his death as being lifted up, the Fourth Gospel is suggesting that in the very act of crucifixion with all of its humiliation, Jesus is honored. It is his glorification. When he is lifted up, Jesus says, his true identity will become clear (8:28), and his departure to his heavenly home will be accomplished (12:34-36).

There are two observations about this theme of being lifted up that merit a slight pause in our hurried pace. First, it is a good example of johannine irony and double-meaning. The fourth evangelist likes to make little word-plays with terms that have double meanings. I call them word-plays, because I think that the evangelist is playing with language. But the point he makes, of course, with this technique is always serious and important. You can almost see him resolving to speak paradoxically as he writes, "When you have lifted up the Son of Man you will know that I am what I am." (8:28) "When you execute me as a common criminal in the most demeaning way, you will bring about my exaltation, the revelation of my true identity." Another example of this use of words with double meaning is in the word *pneuma* in 3:8. It means both "wind" and "spirit." In 3:8 with the use of this one word with two meanings, the evangelist has spun a little metaphor. As the wind moves about freely and uncontrolled by human effort, so does the spirit of God!

A second observation about the theme of the Son of Man's being lifted up: It is the johannine theology of the cross in a nutshell! That is, what John emphasizes throughout his Gospel and specifically in his account of the passion story is that Jesus' death is the revelation of Jesus' identity. Hence, it means that the crucifixion is the honoring of the Son of Man for who he really is. It has been observed many times that Jesus does not comport himself as a victim in the johannine passion story. He does not appear as the one who is suffering disgrace and humiliation. Rather, he behaves as a sovereign and lord of the proceedings. And from the johannine point of view, rightly so, for the passion story in John is the story of the king going to his coronation. It is the account of the anonymous monarch revealing his identity for all his subjects to behold. The consequence is that the humiliation theme is hardly present in the Gospel. If it is present—if Jesus is truly humiliated—it is humiliation which is just the process of exaltation. The Son of Man, the johannine Christ, cannot be humiliated. He is not subject to the decisions of humans, except as he permits it as a means toward his glorification.

The point of this aspect of johannine theology is evident when we compare the Gospel with the point-of-view of Luke. Luke has clearly distinguished the crucifixion and resurrection from the ascension. For a period of forty days the resurrected Christ appears to his disciples (Acts 1:3). Then, as they look on, Christ "was lifted up, and a cloud removed him from their sight" (Acts 1:9). The suggestion of the most of the Gospel of John, on the other hand, is that the crucifixion is that "lifting up." The resurrected Christ is not to be distinguished from the exalted Christ. Crucifixion means exaltation of which resurrection is the expression. Hence, crucifixion and resurrection are bound together in the Gospel of John. The resurrection is in itself the meaning of the crucifixion. Resurrection is the exaltation which crucifixion brings. Consequently, the fourth evangelist has no use for an ascension scene similar to that found in the Acts of the Apostles.

We must confess, however, that the evidence is not quite this neat. There is one passage which seems to speak of an ascension beyond resurrection. The resurrected Christ says to Mary, "Do not cling to me, for I have not yet ascended to the Father" (20:17). That allusion to a future ascension does not fit neatly into the scheme of John's thought as it emerges elsewhere. One is led to suspect that the evangelist is repeating in 20:17 a tradition which came to him. He repeats the allusion to the future ascension of the resurrected Christ, even though his own view is that the ascension has in effect taken place in the crucifixion-resurrection. This demonstrates the manner in which we find contradictions in the thought of the evangelist as a result of his dual efforts to re-present the tradition he knew and to articulate his own thought.

To return again to our delineation of the assertions made about the Son of Man and the Father-Son relationship, the *fifth* is this: The functions of the Son are the functions of God. The Father has given over to the Son those tasks which are usually thought to be preserved for divine prerogative. What the Son does then is what one would usually expect God to do. An example is the matter of judgment. It is the Son who judges on behalf of the Father (3:18; 5:22; 5:27). Likewise, it is the Son of Man (or Son) who is the giver of life (or eternal life) (3:13-15; 6:27; and 6:53). We will discuss the meaning of this pregnant johannine concept of life in the next chapter. But, briefly, it is the gift of authentic existence, the true quality of human existence, or human existence as it was created to be. In John, Jesus is the one who bestows that kind of life. Likewise, it is the Son who reveals the glory of God. In the Old Testament, glory denotes the very presence of God himself. In saying that the Son reveals the glory of God (13:31) the evangelist is asserting that the presence of God is in the presence of Jesus. God's revelation of himself has been delegated to the Son. The Father's work is the work of the Son. But that leads us to a *sixth* point.

The Son carries the full authority of the Father. The Father has placed his "seal of authority" upon the Son (6:27). The authority of the Son is asserted, too, in Jesus' insistence that his glorification is the glorification of the Father (13:31). This matter of divine authority residing in the Son is probably the meaning of that enigmatic statement at 1:51. What does it mean to claim that the disciple will "see heaven wide open and God's angels ascending and descending upon the Son of Man"? It is a difficult concept but it surely means this much: The authority of the divine realm resides in the Son. The Son has clear channels of communication with the Father. If you will, the messengers of God are constantly coming and going in the relationship between the Son and the Father. The Son is then the bearer of divine authority. His words, his acts, and his very person have the force of God himself.

The Father and Son are represented as one yet with distinct individuality. This is our *seventh* point. We have asserted in the discussion of the prologue that it is characteristic johannine christology to say that there is identity between the Father and Christ, yet there is also individuality. That point is borne out by the examination of the passages which speak of the relationship of the Father and Son. On the one hand, there is a series of passages which speak of an identity between the two: 10:30 and 38. It is flatly stated that they are one, and it is further stressed that their works are one: 5:19. They form, as it were, a community of single action. What the Son does is what the Father does. The Son works as the Father directs. So we may conclude that, at least at face value, the Fourth Gospel claims that the Father and Son are one in *being* and in *action*.

On the other hand, there are passages which clearly suggest that there is a distinction between the Father and Son. The Son is said to be obedient to the Father (4:34). Such a statement would suggest that the Son is a separate and free agent who chooses to obey the Father. Obedience implies individuality. Similarly, love implies individuality. The Father loves the Son (3:35). Can there be love unless one supposes a relationship, which in turn implies individuality? Finally, the Father is greater than the Son (14:28). Surely this again suggests individuality. It also articulates an apparent subordination of the Son to the Father which contradicts any conclusion that the Father and Son in the Fourth Gospel are fully one and equal.

I want to avoid saying either that the evangelist was muddle-headed in his description of the Father-Son relation, on the one hand, or that he was a trinitarian theologian, on the other hand. Neither is true. I think he must have known what he was doing in presenting the sayings we have just surveyed. He knew that he was presenting a paradoxical relationship with these passages. But he was no modern theologian concerned to articulate a consistent and logical relationship between the Father and Son. It might well be the case that the evangelist was trying to reconcile divergent factors in his tradition or in his thought.

It is the case, at any rate, that he leaves the reader with a profound paradox. This Son is one with the Father but not identical. He is divine, yet he is in a sense subordinate to God. The evangelist is struggling to define the relationship of the founder of his faith to God, but he has no pat solutions to offer for that relationship. We must admire him for that. What he seems to say is that the Son is the divine agent who participates in the being of the Father and yet who has a distinct individuality of his own.

Our *eighth* point is simpler. The evangelist calls Jesus the "only Son" (3:16 and 18 and possibly 1:18). The Greek word (*monogenēs*) which is translated "only" means "one of its kind." While the evangelist does not make extensive use of this adjective, it seems important that he qualifies the meaning of Son with it on these two or three occasions. What he means by that qualification is possibly to distinguish the sonship of Jesus from any ideas of humans being the sons of God (as they may be the children of God, 1:13). The sonship of the Son of Man, Christ, is absolutely unique. There is none other of comparable nature. Hence, it may also mean that whatever other divine beings there may be, Jesus is superior to them in his unique sonship. The author of Hebrews was concerned to combat some sort of argument that Jesus was just one of the host of angels (chapter 1). Our evangelist again might be responding to Jewish charges that the Jesus whom Christians call Messiah is at best an angel. Not so, responds the evangelist. He is God's unique, one-of-a-kind Son.

Finally, it is obvious that the fourth evangelist wants his reader to get one message loud and clear. That message is this: To respond to Jesus, the Son, is to respond to God, the Father (5:23). The point of the discussions of the identity of the johannine Jesus is not a purely theological one when it comes right down to it. The point the evangelist is making is a practical one. However you define the specific relationship between the Son and the Father, how you respond to the Son constitutes your response to God. Accept him and you have accepted God. Reject him and you have rejected God. It is as if the evangelist is saying, "Well, I am not enough of a theologian to say any more than what I have about the relationship of the Son and the Father. But of this much we Christians are sure: Your relationship with Christ comprises your relationship with God." Coming out of this christological discussion then is a pragmatic point.

It is obvious, then, that sonship of the Fourth Gospel means a unique relationship with God by one who himself participates in God's very being (and hence is divine). I might add in way of conclusion to this section that again John's christology is a creative wedding of two different themes. In Jewish thought to be a son of God was primarily a matter of obedience. To be obedient to God made one a son of God. Even today the expression *bar mitzvah* means that one is a son of the commandment when one takes up those commandments in obedience. But sonship of the diety in hellenistic thought was a cosmic or ontological matter. To be the Son of God was to have the nature of diety in one's person. The sons of God were mythologically begotten by the gods. Hence, hellenistic divine sonship was a matter of the essence of the person, while Jewish divine sonship was a matter of the function or behavior of the person. The evangelist has portrayed Jesus as the Father's Son in a way which bridges the difference. Jesus is the Father's Son most certainly by virtue of his obedience to the Father (4:34). But he is more. His very essence is the essence of the Father (10:30). We do not want to impose later essentialistic language upon our evangelist. But we may credit him with perceiving the difference between the meaning of sonship in hellenistic and Jewish thought and then proceeding in his explication of Jesus to make his sonship the fulfillment of both.

D. THE CHRISTOLOGICAL MEANING OF THE "I AM" SAYINGS

Reader's Preparation: Here are the most significant passages in which the "I am" expression appears in the Greek.

a) Without a predicate: 8:24; 8:28; 8:58; 13:19.

b) With an implied predicate: 6:20 and 18:5.

c) With an explicit predicate: 6:35; 6:51; 8:12; 8:18; 8:23; 9:5; 10:7; 10:9; 10:11; 10:14; 11:25; 14:6; 15:1; 15:5; (Possibly 4:26).

It may help you to read the following revisions of some of the New English Bible translations. I have translated the Greek "I am" construction more literally here to help you spot it.

8:24—"If you do not believe that *I am*, you will die in your sins."

8:28—"When you have lifted up the Son of Man you will know that *I am*.

13:19—"I tell you this now, before the event, that when it happens you may believe that *I am*."

6:20—"He called out, '*I am*; do not be afraid.'"

18:5—"Jesus said, '*I am*.'"

8:18—"*I am* the one who testifies concerning myself."

8:23—"*I am* from above. Your home is in this world; *I am* not from this world.

The johannine Christ is the eternal Word of God who has become incarnate. He is all that the Jewish Messiah is but more, namely, the Son of Man. As Son of Man, or the Father's Son, he is one who fully participates in the being of God and yet has individuality from the Father. To this picture of Christ in the Fourth Gospel we must add still another element. That is the christological meaning of the enigmatic "I am" sayings. These sayings should be investigated from several different angles, but this brief introductory glimpse will be concerned only with what they suggest about the view of Christ in the Fourth Gospel.

First of all, what is an "I am" saying? It is a purported word of Jesus in which an emphatic construction (*ego eimi*) appears in the Greek. The normal way in which one would write "I am" in koine Greek (the form of Greek in which the New Testament was written) is *eimi*. For emphasis one might add the first person pronoun, *ego*. The result is literally something like, "I, myself am!" But we will see that the peculiar construction seems to have meaning beyond a simple emphasis upon the pronoun.

This emphatic construction appears in three ways in the Fourth Gospel on the lips of Jesus: "I am" with an explicit predicate. An example is 6:35: "I am the bread of life." Another form is the 'I am" with what appears to be an implied predicate. An example of this form is 6:20. The translation in the New English Bible quite correctly supplies the predicate in its rendering, "It is I." The Greek however reads simply, *ego eimi*, "I am." The sense of these formulations with an implied predicate may very well be something like, "I am he," but the emphatic form suggests the evangelist has something special in mind. That special meaning is obviously intended in the so-called absolute "I am" sayings, those without any predicate either implicit or explicit. 8:24 will serve as our example here: "If you do not believe that I am what I am, you will die in your sins." Again the New English Bible has helped the reader by supplying a predicate ("what I am"). That hypothetical predicate may be quite appropriate. But the Greek reads, "If you do not believe that I am, you will die in your sins." (An example from the synoptic Gospels is Mark 14:62 and Luke 22:70.)

Most interpreters of the Fourth Gospel agree that the "I am" sayings are more than simple emphatic statements. They believe that the Fourth Gospel uses this formulation in a profound christological way. The heart of the problem is the absolute "I am" sayings (those without predicates). The meaning of the absolute form may suggest the meaning of those with both explicit and implicit predicates.

The meaning of the "I am" sayings may be hinted at in the affinity they have with similar kinds of sayings in other religious traditions. It is commonly recognized that among certain of the religions of the hellenistic world of the first century the revealer gods spoke with the emphatic *ego eimi*. The god Isis is quoted in inscriptions using the "I am" saying with predicates. (See Howard Clark Kee's *The Origins of Christianity: Sources and Documents*, pages 83-84.) Similarly, parallels can be found in that body of literature called the Hermetic Corpus, particularly where Poimandres reveals himself to Hermes. Others have claimed that the Mandean literature is relevant. That literature actually dates much later than the first century, A.D., but it is argued that the religious movement dated from a time contemporaneous with the origin of Christianity. The Mandaean literature contains passages which seem to have parallel "I am" constructions. Most of these parallels in hellenistic religions are comparable to the johannine sayings in which a predicate follows the "I am." For instance, in the Hermetical literature the following can be found: "the messenger of light am I" and "the treasure am I, the treasure of life." Or, in the Mandaean literature: "A shepherd am I, who loves his sheep" and "a fisherman am I who. . . ." (These examples are drawn for the most part from Bultmann's commentary on the Fourth Gospel.)

It appears then that there was a precedent in hellenistic religious thought and practice for attributing to the god such emphatic "I am" sayings—at least in their form with a predicate. Some believe that the "I am" sayings in the Fourth Gospel are intentionally modeled after these uses in hellenistic religions. Further they suggest that the fourth evangelist is asserting the identity of Christ in contrast to some of the claims of hellenistic gods. Hence, when he has Jesus saying emphatically, "I am the good shepherd" (10:14), he intends to contrast Christ with other claims for divine status in the hellenistic world. Whether or not such a contrast is intended, it is clear that hellenistic religions offer a precedent for the revealer god using the emphatic "I am." Such a statement on the lips of the god signaled the utterance of a revelation of the truth which the god had to offer.

When we turn in the direction of the Old Testament and Jewish religion for a precedent for the "I am " saying, we find there something like the absolute "I am." The hellenistic literature seems to offer parallels only for the "I am" speeches with predicates. But not so the Old Testament. If you remember your Old Testament, you will recall the meaning of the sacred name for God revealed to Moses in Exodus 3:14. It is difficult to say how the Hebrew there should be translated. But one of the most likely translations reads, "I AM: that is who I am. Tell them that I AM has sent you to them." Could it be that the fourth evangelist intends to stir in the reader a recognition that the sacred name for God, YHWH, meant quite literally, "I am"?

The pursuit of Old Testament and Jewish parallels gets hotter when we turn to the Greek translation of the Old Testament. This translation (called the Septuagint, or LXX) was the popular Old Testament used among Greek-speaking Jews and Christians in the first century. We find that in any number of passages the translators have used the emphatic *ego eimi* to render the original Hebrew. In a number of places the Hebrew which reads something like "I, Yahweh" is translated by the LXX, "I am" (*ego eimi*—Isaiah 41:4, 45:18, Hosea 13:4, and Joel 2:27). In Isaiah a number of passages in which the Hebrew reads "I, I am He . . . ," the Greek translation is "I am I am." These Old Testament passages all have to do with the direct speaking of God. They all emphasize the oneness of God and his existence. (Thanks to Raymond Brown for his excellent appendix on the "I am" sayings in his commentary on John, volume I.)

Out of these sketchy allusions to the possible precedents for the use of the "I am" formulation in religious literature of the first century, we can begin to construct the meaning the fourth evangelist intends. First, we can claim with some degree of safety, I think, that the evangelist means the "I am " formulation to signal the speaking of God. Out of both the hellenistic and Old Testament-Jewish backgrounds he drew the idea of the use of this construction in connection with the divine revelation. In other words, the occurrence of this construction marks a theophany—the appearance and revelation (speaking) of God. The fourth evangelist intends to use a formula which sets off the sirens in the minds of both his hellenistic and Jewish Christian readers. When either read that stately, "I am," he thought of the revelation of the divine to the human.

Second, I think we can conclude that the evangelist was making an exclusive claim for Christ with the use of the "I am" sayings. Maybe the contrast with other religious claims is implicit in some of the "I am" sayings with predicates like "the good shepherd" and "the bread of life." The fourth evangelist is saying that whatever other claims you have heard, Jesus is the true divine revealer. Hence, I think he is aware of the use of the *ego eimi* in hellenistic religions. But that claim for the exclusive truth of Christ also roots in the Old Testament and Jewish tradition. He is saying that just as Yahweh is the one true God, so Christ is the one true divine revealer. None other is comparable.

Finally, it is likely that the sound of those words "I am" in the locale of the evangelist meant the very name of God. That name could not be uttered. Jewish piety had long forbidden the pronouncing of the sacred name, YHWH. So, when Jesus is made to say "I am," it is the very name of God himself Jesus is uttering. The implication is that he himself *is* God. He may allow that sacred name to pass from his lips, because he is the one whom the name designates. As Yahweh in the Old Testament speaks his own name, so Christ may speak that divine name. If this is so, then we have here one of the highest claims for Christ's divinity in the entire New Testament. If this is so, we have an unequivocal indication that the fourth evangelist held Christ to be God himself, or least so far as practical human matters were concerned.

In summary, the fourth evangelist employs this tantalizing Greek construction in full knowledge of its religious significance, both hellenistic and Jewish. He employs it to assert the divinity of the founder of his faith. He uses it to claim that that founder is the only source of truth and full human existence. And he uses it to claim that, when Christ speaks, it is God who speaks. All of this seems quite consistent with the view of Jesus we have seen emerging in the other parts of the Gospel. It is consistent with the prologue of the gospel, with the insistence of the evangelist that Christ is more than the Jewish Messiah, and with the Son of Man and Father-Son relationship passages. What it does is to underline the *functional equivalency* of God and Christ. That is, it says in effect that so far as human concerns go, Christ and God are one and the same. The words of Christ are God's words. The actions of Christ are God's actions. The human response to Christ is the response to God. For all human purposes, then, the Christ figure is God. But the fourth evangelist does this consistently. Now the mysterious "I am" formula furthers that point. But we must draw all this together now in a conclusion.

E. CONCLUSION

The fourth evangelist has expressed a clear view of the founder of the Christian movement. He has taken the Christian experience of the founder as his primary evidence for the formulation of his view. That is, what he says about the Christ figure is an effort to say what it is that the Christians experience in their community of faith. We might confront him with the charge that he is dealing in speculation. He has taken a simple historical figure, the man Jesus of Nazareth, and made him into something that he was not. John's response I think we can construct with a little imagination. He would say that the community of faith with which he is associated knows this man Jesus in a different way. They know him as one who has brought a totally new orientation to life. Their faith in him has brought them what they consider to be the true essence of human life—eternal life, if you will. They know their founder not as one buried in history but as a living presence communicated to them through the activity of the Spirit. (See chapter four.) Hence, the author of our gospel is not speculating, he would claim. He is not distorting history. Rather, he understood what he was doing as an articulation of reality as experienced by the community of faith of which he was a member.

The founder of that faith was none other than the Father's Son, claims the Fourth Gospel. This means that the evangelist along with his community had concluded that one who could communicate truth in the way that Christ had brought them to truth could be no other than Gòd himself. It was a quality of truth which could not be communicated secondhand. It was not a truth that had been filtered through a human prophet. Divine truth had been communicated to Israel and to persons of the hellenistic world through human prophets and revealers. But the reality which the community of faith had found in the revelation attributed to this man Jesus was of another quality. It was the "real thing." It was directly encountered in Christ. No intermediary could be responsible for this truth. Otherwise, how could it have so radically turned the believers around, so radically altered their lives?

So, the evangelist states flatly and unashamedly that it is *only* in this Christ figure that one finds the divine reality. He is the true bread, the light, the life, the resurrection, and the way of authentic human life. The fourth evangelist brings this exclusivism to its epitome in the assertion which he places on the lips of Jesus, "No one comes to the Father except by me" (14:6). Such a claim for exclusive access to the Ultimate Reality startles the modern mind. It sounds dogmatic and narrow. It can only be understood in the context of a community of faith for whom their founder has been the avenue of a new relationship with that Ultimate Reality.

But the evangelist recognizes that their founder is the Father's *Son*. All of the statements which assert the divinity of Christ are qualified by the fact that he is the Father's Son, not the Father himself. The fourth evangelist was no systematic theologian, as we have said several times. But he was theologically sophisticated enough to make clear that Christ was not God himself. The author of our gospel and his community seem to have held that Christ was divine—participated in the being of God—but was distinct and, I believe, subordinate to the Father. He was the expressive dimension of God's being, or the Son who is fully obedient to the Father. Our evangelist recognizes that whatever the incarnation of the Logos means it cannot mean that a human being is in every way fully the being of God. Had he known the concept of the self-emptying (*kenosis*) of Christ found in the Philippian christological hymn (2:7), he might well have employed it. As it is, he claims in a paradoxical manner the divinity of Christ, yet his individuality, distinctiveness, and subordination to the Father. In other words, Christ is the Father's Son.

To say it another way, the fourth evangelist claims that Christ is the functional equivalent of God. In being, the two may be distincv. But in practice they are one. So far as human beings are concerned, Christ is God in their midst. We are thus led to acknowledge that the evangelist's main concern is not the construction of theological doctrine but rather the support of practical faith. He is concerned to articulate a point-of-view which is pragmatic, useful. In practice the Christian may think of Christ as God in their midst. The reason for this claim is that it is the real experience of the Christian community to which the evangelist belonged.

The religious experience of the Christian community is thus the first basis upon which the evangelist formulated his theology. The second is the opposition the church faced from the synagogue. He is reacting to the charges brought against the Christians in their city. They are charged with worshipping two Gods. Their Christ is declared to be less than divine by their opponents. He was an angel, a prophet, or maybe even a pretender to the messianic throne. But he is certainly not Messiah or divine. John structures a response to these charges. He tries to formulate a view of Christ which claims that Christ was the Messiah, was divine, and yet does not represent a second God. How well he succeeds at this task we leave to your judgment. But it is important to see the christology of the Fourth Gospel in the context of this combat between the church and its opponents.

It is fair, then, to say that the christology of the Gospel is reactionary. It is the reaction to the assault of the opponents. It states its case as a response. In realizing this, we are helped to understand the exclusivism of the johannine community. That exclusive claim for Christ which we witnessed in the section on the "I am" sayings is due to the church's situation at the time. The church is in a defensive posture; it is struggling for its survival against a formidable foe. And religious communities in this kind of a situation often state their case in the most radical form.

Consequently, the christology of the Fourth Gospel is a concept fashioned out of a real, lived situation. These two aspects of that situation are vital for our understanding of the evangelist: The church's profound faith experience of Christ and its intense struggle with local opponents. The christology of the Gospel is then an admirable example of the community's effort to think amid a concrete situation in a new way about its founder. We may feel that the view of Christ represented in the Fourth Gospel needs to be balanced by the perspectives of the other Gospels as well as by the later thought of the church. And we may even want to question John's understanding of the early Christian experience itself. Nevertheless, we can still understand his concerns and appreciate why he said what he did. We can empathize with his situation, and we can appreciate his response to the issues. In a faithful and creative way, he rethought the answers to fundamental questions which had been raised regarding the nature and function of the founder of the Christian movement, and he did this in light of what believers were currently experiencing. In this he did what each constructive religious thinker must do in every period of history and what we too must often do ourselves.

2. Two Different Worlds—
Johannine Dualism

WHY IS THERE EVIL? WHY DO HUMANS continually encounter that which is senseless and wasteful of human life? Why do good people suffer for no apparent reason? Why are there earthquakes, storms, and other forms of natural destruction? If much of the undesirable aspect of life can be blamed upon human ignorance and immaturity, what about that dimension of nature which strikes us as senseless? How can one account for that? What explanation can be offered to the whole reality of evil?

Of course, all persons throughout history have encountered these questions. It can even be said that one of the most important dimensions of religious thought has been the attempt either to understand or to come to terms with the problem of evil. The simplest religious explanation was to attribute evil to the action of the gods. It was the manifestation of their wrath, and if humans were to escape destruction they must somehow appease the divine wrath. From the simplest of religious explanations of evil to the more complex, religious systems have offered their adherents ways of dealing with this puzzling dimension of human existence. The various ways of handling evil within religious systems are numerous. In some religions evil is simply illusion. It is only the appearnace of reality, and salvation consists of that insight which enlightens apparent evil for what it really is (e.g., especially Hinduism). For others evil is very real. It is the result of some suprahuman will which opposes the divine will. That opposition wreaks disaster and distress throughout the course of world history, but will finally be overcome at the conclusion of history (e.g., Zoroastrianism). Even in those systems of human thought and action which are only quasi-religious, there is an effort to deal with the reality of evil. It is a part of the rhythm of nature (e.g., Confucianism), or it is the result entirely of human decisions (e.g., humanism).

Hence, the question of evil is no simple intellectual puzzle for idle speculators. It is a basic human problem which is encountered by every person sooner or later. Its difficulty is not simply an academic matter, but one which roots at the core of human personality. It is, if you will, a *lived* problem. That is, it is one which we experience directly and forcefully. The reality of evil rocks us and shakes the foundations of our confidence in the meaningfulness of existence. It touches all of our lives. One need not be a religious person to wrestle with the radically undesirable experiences of life and still go on affirming that life is worthwhile.

Early Christianity inherited a modified dualism from its parent body, Judaism. In the five centuries before the birth of Christianity, Judaism had developed an understanding of evil which was essentially dualistic. It held that there was an opposing supra-human force which thwarted the divine will. That opposition, however, was understood to be short-lived. Its days were numbered, for in a climactic event in which the long-awaited Messiah would appear, all opposition to the sovereign Lord of creation would be overcome. God would again reign supreme in his world. But, in the meantime, the force of evil was not only very real but even prominent. The early Christians apparently believed that in the events of the life of Jesus of Nazareth the powerful rule of Satan was decisively defeated. The second appearance of Christ from the heavens would bring the annihilation of all semblances of evil. Hence, these early Christians conceived of themselves as living in the interim period between the first appearance of Christ and the defeat of evil, on the one side, and his second appearance which would actualize the elimination of all traces of evil, on the other. Their belief was then a limited dualism in the sense that the forces of evil were not ultimately as powerful as God and would eventually cease to exist.

Theirs was also a dualism of time. History was divided into two basic periods—the present era still dominated by the power of Satan and the age to come in which Satan and his force would be destroyed and God's reign actualized. We might like to think of this double dualism in the following way. The vertical dimension represents a cosmic dualism, and the horizontal dimension a temporal (or historical) dualism:

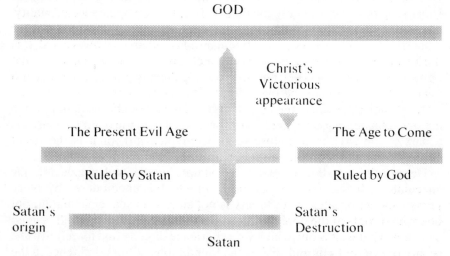

GOD

Christ's
Victorious
appearance

The Present Evil Age   The Age to Come

Ruled by Satan   Ruled by God

Satan's   Satan's
origin   Destruction

Satan

Our Fourth Gospel characteristically does not accept this view in total. It presents a revision of the dualistic thought of the New Testament in general. It is, on the one hand, the most dualistic of the New Testament literature; on the other hand, it is not a continuation of this early Christian view. We need to discuss the revisions of early Christian thought at the hand of the fourth evangelist under two general topics. In this chapter we will discuss johannine dualism in general. But later on (chapter four) we will find it necessary to return to this theme when we attempt to understand johannine eschatology.

For now, we will have our work cut out for us if we can grasp how the fourth evangelist uses dualistic symbols. Hence, we will divide our discussion into three sections:

1. The dualistic symbols of the Fourth Gospel,
2. The peculiar attitude of the Gospel toward "The Jews," and
3. The question of predeterminism in the Gospel.

> *Reader's Preparation*: Skim through the Gospel still another time. This time try to find and list all of the pairs of opposites which appear in the Gospel. Sometimes you may sense that a word or pharse is used to mean either the negative or positive side of a pair, but not find the explicit use of the opposite member. List these as well. An example of what you are looking for are the "light-darkness" opposites.

A. THE DUALISTIC SYMBOLS OF THE FOURTH GOSPEL

You should not have to read far into the Gospel before you are struck with the writer's use of dualistic symbols. The prologue of the Gospel presents us with the dualism of the light and the darkness. "The light shines on in the dark, and the darkness has never quenched it." (1:5) Of course, such pairs of opposites are not unusual in the New Testament or in the Old Testament. What is unusual in our Gospel is the prominence of these pairs. It would appear that the whole religious system of thought presented in the Fourth Gospel hangs within a framework of a dualism. That dualism constitutes the two anchoring points between which the writer has woven his thought. The following is only a partial list of some of the most obvious pairs of opposite symbols employed by the evangelist. Your list hopefully will include several that this abbreviated chart omits. Write in your additions.

POSITIVE POLE	EXAMPLE	NEGATIVE POLE
light	1:5	darkness
above	8:23	below
spirit	3:6	flesh
life (eternal)	3:36	death
truth	8:44f.	falsehood (lie)
heaven	3:31	earth
God	13:27	Satan
Israel	1:19 and 47	"The Jews" (sometimes)
	17:14	the world (sometimes)

Let us now try to explore the meaning of this dualism. We will attempt to do so through the investigation of one of the very important johannine symbols, "world" *(kosmos)*. First, we will try to ascertain what the evangelist means by this term and characterize its role in his dualistic system. Second, we will use the meaning we find in the uses of "world" to make some general assertions about johannine dualism. We choose this concept of the world because it is so crucial to the thought of the Gospel and because it exemplifies the complex way in which the evangelist uses his symbols.

> *Reader's Preparation:* You should try to catch the flavor of the way in which the fourth evangelist uses this term, world. The following are some of the passages you might read and ponder. Ask yourself, "What does he mean by 'world' in each of these cases?" 1:10; 3:16; 8:12; 8:23; 9:29-41; 11:9-10; 12:25; 12:31-33; 12:46; 13:1; 14:17; 14:31; 16:7-11; 18:36.

First, we must note that John's use of the term *kosmos* is not consistent. We have listed it above as one of the symbols used for the negative pole of his dualism. And that it is, *sometimes*. But the reader of the Gospel must watch the context in which this (and other key terms) is used, for it can have a variety of meanings.

In a number of passages this term is employed in a neutral or even positive sense. There it means the creation itself—the physical reality of this earth. Read 17:24; 16:21; 1:9; and 3:16. These are occurrences of the term in at least a neutral sense. This should tell us something important as we prepare to examine the passages where the term is used in a negative, dualistic sense. It should inform us that the writer of the Gospel does not have a negative view of the physical world itself. That is, when he does use *kosmos* in a negative, dualistic sense, he is not referring to this physical world in which we live. This is so because he has, in the passages just cited, used *kosmos* in an essentially neutral sense. This created earth is not the negative meaning of the term *kosmos,* for it is the object of God's love (3:16). It is the realm in which the light enlightens persons (1:9). Some Christian interpretations in past years have seriously misunderstood the Gospel at this point. They have taken the fourth evangelist to be depreciating the physical world. Hence they understand that he calls upon the Christian disciple to be only remotely in contact with the materiality of this earth (e.g., 17:18). This is a gross distortion of johannine thought, for there are these passages in which "world" is used to refer in an approving way to this physical earth.

So, what does the writer mean when he uses this term in a negative way? The world, in these cases, seems to be a symbol to represent the realm of unbelief, the realm in which there is total rejection of the truth of God revealed in Christ. It is used in conjunction with judgment and with Satan in

9:39; 12:31; and 16:11. It symbolizes that way of being—that way of living—which is opposed to God and His plan of salvation for humans. It is a stance in life which finds relationship with God unnecessary and undesirable. It is then what Bultmann has called "the perversion of creation." "The delusion that arises from the will to exist of and by one's self perverts the truth into a lie, perverts the creation into the 'world'" (*Theology of the New Testament*, vol. II, 29). Creation means the necessity of human dependence upon God. The "world" symbolizes the pretense that human existence can be independent of God. It is a way of living in which the human tries to be something he or she is not, namely, an independent being having no need of the One responsible for existence.

If this is a correct interpretation of the johannine meaning, then it is implied that creation is a correct, authentic way of being human, while the world represents an inauthentic, "phoney" way of conceiving of oneself. This is not basically a moral distinction between those who live "good lives" as opposed to those who live "bad lives." It is a distinction between two ways of understanding oneself in relationship to the whole of reality. It is a distinction between two ways in which a person might answer the question, "Who am I?" So the world in johannine usage is tied to the negative poles of his dualism. The world is darkness (8:12). It is ruled by Satan (12:31).

But we have yet to wrestle with the fully dualistic uses of the term. In 8:23 and 13:1, for instance, this world is set over against another realm. In both cases the point is that Jesus' home is not this world but another. "Your home is in this world, mine is not." (8:23) "Jesus knew that his hour had come and he must leave this world and go to the Father." (13:1) Here the world is a realm of being distinct from the realm of the divine, and it would seem that this distinction is synonymous with several others in the Fourth Gospel: for instance, earth and heaven and below and above. The realm of the divine is other than this world. That realm is elsewhere. Jesus' home is in that other realm, and he comes into the worldly realm only temporarily. The distinction is then between the world as the human-natural realm over against the uncreated, divine realm. The first is dependent and created, while the second is independent and uncreated.

This use of the world as a realm distinct from the heavenly realm along with the use of other polarities like above and below, heaven and earth suggests an important point. It would seem that the fourth evangelist embraced a cosmic dualism of two worlds. Much of the New Testament literature implies a kind of three-story universe: God and the angels in the highest level, Satan and the demons in the lowest, and humans with nature stuck between the two. But nowhere else is the cosmic dualism so evident as it is in the Fourth Gospel. Some scholars have suggested that in the Fourth Gospel the historical dualism of early Christian thought (the horizontal dimension of the diagram used above) has been entirely transposed into a cosmic dualism (the vertical dimension of our diagram). Part of the reason for

saying this is that almost all of the references to the historical eschatology
are absent from John's Gospel. That is, the allusion to the end of the present
age and the commencement of the age to come (the eternal age) are
conspicuously missing in the Fourth Gospel. In their place, say these
scholars, stands the radical cosmic dualism. If this is so, then the fourth
evangelist has de-temporalized the historical dualism of early Christianity
and produced a cosmic dualism. (See chapter four for further discussion of
this possibility.)

We are still faced with some difficulties, however. Let us grant that there
is some truth to the suggestion that the temporal dualism has been transposed into a cosmic one in the Fourth Gospel. (Remnants of the temporal
division are still to be found in the Fourth Gospel, however.) What then is
the relationship of this cosmic dualism to the dualism of human self-
understanding which we mentioned earlier? We have the division of persons among those who live authentically as creatures of God and those who
live inauthentically as if they were independent of God. Is that dualism
different from the cosmic dualism of the world above and the world below
which we have just encountered? Or, to pose the question differently, how
literally did the fourth evangelist and his church embrace this cosmic
dualism? Did they really believe in two different worlds?

There are two possibilities, I think: One is that we have in the Fourth
Gospel two kinds of dualism both represented in the use of the word, world.
A human dualism—two ways of self-understanding—and a cosmic dualism—two realms of being. In this case we would want to read the cosmic
dualism rather literally. We might suggest that for this way of understanding
John the cosmic dualism would be almost a kind of Platonic division of
reality. The other possibility is that the cosmic dualism represents another
way of stating the human dualism. That is, the two different worlds—the
world of the human and the world of the divine—are picture language to say
that persons may choose to understand themselves either as independent of
God or as dependent creatures. The fourth evangelist would, in this case,
not mean that there are literally two different realms within this cosmos.
Rather, he means that those two realms are a poetic way of expressing the
conviction that humans must choose to live either under the rule of God or
try to escape that rule. The two-story cosmos of John would then be a
metaphor for human lifestyles.

Here, I think, we are up against a very difficult matter. It is difficult, because our choice between these two interpretations of the cosmic dualism
calls for a basic understanding of how the evangelist used his symbols. We
are wedded to a distinction between literal and poetic description. Modern
science in all disciplines (history as well as biology, for instance) has helped
us to try to keep separate the times when we want to describe reality exactly as it is (or as exactly as possible) and the times we wish to reflect upon the

meaning of reality for us. So we talk about "facts" and objective reality, on the one hand, and poetry or subjective understanding, on the other. We keep these distinct. We don't want the biologist telling us how she or he *feels* about the little living creatures being studied; we want her or him to describe that form of life to us as exactly as possible. But when we read poetry or a novel we have no expectation that its assertions are "scientific."

Now this distinction is a modern one. It is one which our evangelist did not know. The first century Christians did not carefully divide descriptive history from interpretative history. The writers of the New Testament could flow from fact to subjective meaning and back again to fact without any break and without any concern to delineate the difference. Therefore, myth and objective truth are mixed in early Christian literature. Picture language and descriptive language are found within the same sentence.

All this means that our evangelist might not have made the distinction we are trying to make in his dualistic symbols. Do they describe the cosmos, or do they describe the way he believed persons must decide how to understand themselves? He probably did not think this way. If the cosmic dualism is really a picture language about human self-understanding, the evangelist probably did not consciously think of it this way. This is not to say that he was any less sophisticated than we, but only that he wrote in a pre-scientific age. We must not expect him to make the same distinctions in his kinds of language that we would make.

I am inclined to think that his human dualism is continuous with his cosmic dualism. He wants to make the point primarily that humans are faced with two possibilities. His cosmic dualism enters into his language for two reasons: One, to reinforce the importance of the human dualism. I maintain again that the reference to the divine, other realm here, as in christology, is a signal of the existential importance the matter carried for the evangelist and his church. Two, he introduces it to tie it to his christology. Christ is from the realm of self-understanding which is divinely oriented. This world *(kosmos)* continues to represent the other phoney kind of human self-understanding. But having said that, I would not want to deny that the evangelist might have sincerely believed in a kind of two-story cosmos. He very well might have. What I think he would say, however, is that your belief in the structure of the cosmos is not the important thing. The vital issue is whether you will accept yourself as God's creature and all that that implies, or whether you will try to pretend that you can live in independence from God as if your life were your own doing.

Reader's Preparation: Now read some passages where other pairs of opposites are used or implied and see what meaning they seem to have. 1:4-5; 3:1-21; 3:31-36; 8:21-26; 9:5; 13:27-30.

We now have the key to unlock the mysteries of other johannine dualistic symbols. There is a negative pole which describes the state of human life which is misdirected and confused. That state is described variously as darkness, falsehood, flesh, death, Satan's realm, and the below. Even the evangelist's use of "night" may suggest the darkness which characterizes erroneous human self-understanding (13:30). The positive pole of the split is symbolized as light, truth, spirit, life and eternal life, God's rule, the above. Again we have a double dualism—a cosmic division of all reality into two realms, the created and the divine (especially, 8:23), and a division among ways of being human, best expressed, perhaps, in the truth-falsehood dualism. The various symbols all mean the same thing. There is no essential difference between the dualism of light and darkness and the split of the above and the below. The positive pole of the split represents one point: God's revelation of himself in Christ which enables persons to become who they really are. Truth means the truth which saves humans from a misguided, contorted existence. It is God's love, according to the fourth evangelist, which motivates him to reveal to humans their true being. If a child for some reason thinks of himself as a dog, the concerned father does all he can to correct the child's misunderstanding of himself. God is doing nothing else in his effort to demonstrate to humans that they are his creatures and dependent upon him for their existence.

The johannine dualism of two different worlds is then the evangelist's understanding of the human need for salvation and the nature of that salvation. It is his way of saying that all the evil of the world roots in a misconstrued self-understanding. The darkness and falsehood of this world result because persons try to be other than what they are. That sounds amazingly simple, but it seems to be the johannine view of the matter. Why is there evil? Because humans are confused as to their identity. How is evil overcome? By humans correcting their faulty understanding of themselves. The two different worlds of John are two different identities!

We may summarize this view of johannine dualism by means of a simple diagram. The form of the diagram is intended to suggest that the evangelist's human dualism flows into his cosmic dualism and that the latter is really in final analysis an expression of the former:

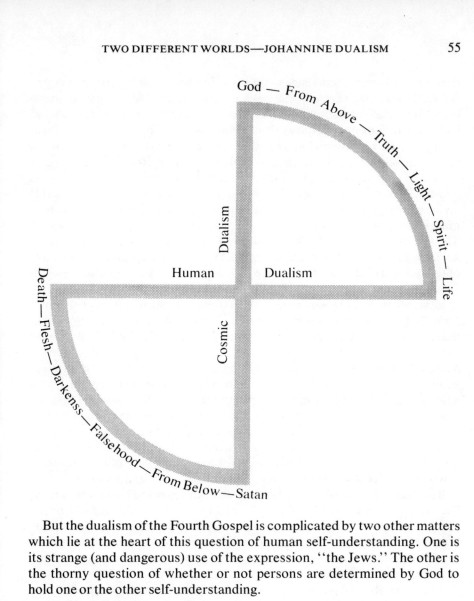

But the dualism of the Fourth Gospel is complicated by two other matters which lie at the heart of this question of human self-understanding. One is its strange (and dangerous) use of the expression, "the Jews." The other is the thorny question of whether or not persons are determined by God to hold one or the other self-understanding.

B. "THE JEWS" IN THE FOURTH GOSPEL

> *Reader's Preparation*: Skim through the Gospel and mark all the appearances of the use of the expression, "the Jews." Try to decide in which cases it is used a neutral way to designate an ethnic group of people and when it is used in a pejorative manner. You might compare the way the term is used in chapters 11 and 12 as opposed to chapter 8.

One of the strange facts about this gospel is that while the synoptic Gospels each refer to the Jews five or six times, the fourth evangelist has over seventy such occurrences. On the other hand, the common synoptic distinctions among scribes, pharisees and sadducees is found less frequently in John. The manner in which the Fourth Gospel refers to the Jews has had some tragic consequences. It has been used again and again as a basis for a Christian anti-Semitism. No other Gospel appears to place the Jews so radically over against the Christians as their enemies. Hence, those persons in need of a scapegoat group for their hostility have seized upon the apparent anti-Jewishness of the Gospel. They have used it as a rationale for a belief in divine wrath against the Jews. On the other hand, those Christians concerned to wipe out all traces of anti-Semitism are embarrassed by the Fourth Gospel. The use of the term, "the Jews," in the Fourth Gospel has had important social ramifications, but it also has importance in the general understanding of the religious thought of this Gospel. That gives us two important reasons for trying to get behind the evangelist's use of this expression.

First, we must note again that John's use of the term is not consistent. I hope that you found in your reading the fact that the term is ambiguous— that it seems to be used one way here and another there. Let's deal with the easy one first. Sometimes it is used simply to identify a group of persons— nationally, ethnically, and religiously. In 11:45, for instance, the term appears simply to identify a group from which some believers in Christ emerged. In 4:22 Jesus is made to say (speaking as a Jew himself) that it is from the Jews that salvation comes. This is supplemented by the fact that the mighty figures of Judaism's past are recognized to be important forerunners of the revealer (5:46 and 8:39). With this we have no problem. It represents the Jews as the preparation for the appearance of the johannine Christ and suggests the continuity of early Christianity and Judaism.

But the knotty problem arises when we encounter the polemic sounding uses of the expression. The Jews are almost always the villains in the Gospel. They persecute Jesus (5:16); they misunderstand him (8:22); they attempt to stone him (8:59); they are responsible for his arrest and crucifixion (18:12 and 19:12). Most characteristically they are the ones who refuse to believe in him (10:31ff.).

Raymond Brown presents a cogent argument for why we cannot read these polemical passages as referring in general to the Jewish people. First, the term, "the Jews," often has nothing to do with religious, national, or ethnic considerations. The parents of the blind man in chapter nine are afraid of the "Jews," but they themselves are surely Jews! Second, the expression is often used interchangeably with the religious leaders of the people (compare 18:3 with 18:12 and 8:13 with 8:18ff.). Third, when we compare the Fourth Gospel with the Synoptics, "the Jews" perform those functions which in the Synoptics are assigned to the Sanhedrin (John 18:28-31 compared with Mark 15:1). It is Brown's contention then that the "Jews" is an expression used to designate only the religious authorities of Judaism who are opposed to Christ. (See Brown's commentary, vol. I, p. lxxi.)

I would want to suggest a somewhat broader meaning for the expression in the Fourth Gospel. It is the religious authorities, to be sure, who are often referred to with the expression, the Jews, but it is also a wider class of opponents. The Jews are *stylized types* of those who reject Christ. The Jews are a type of person for the evangelist, and it is that which motivates his strange category. They lose their specific ethnic characteristic in the Fourth Gospel. It is no longer a religious body of persons designated by this term, because John has so used it as to make them simply a type, not a specific person.

Let me suggest an analogy. In the sundry adventure and mystery stories involving private investigators, the official police play a consistent role. They are always rather dull, slow, bogged down in redtape, and easily thrown off the scent. They are a foil with which the writer demonstrates the skill and brilliance of the private detective, the writer's hero. We can say that in these stories the police have become *stylized types*. They have no distinctive personalities. The author is not interested in them except for one reason, namely, as a contrast to his hero. Hence, there is in this literary and media genre a massive generalization.

The analogy helps us understand what the fourth evangelist has done with the Jews. He is not interested in them as a people. He does not distinguish characters among them. He is interested in them only as *types of unbelief*. They are his foil over against his hero, the divine revealer. They function only so as to give the evangelist a chance to say what he wants to say about Christ. Hence, we must not conclude that he had an anti-Semitic motif in mind. We do not say that the author of the private detective story is an anti-establishment, anti-police revolutionary. Neither can we accuse our author of being anti-Semitic.

But why have the Jews been chosen for this unseemly role? We must recall some suggestions made in the Introduction. Remember that the evangelist is writing amid a ferocious dialogue with the synagogue—one which doubtless had erupted into violence from time to time. The immediate problem for the johannine community is the attack from the Jewish synagogue. For this reason, the fourth evangelist takes out of his immediate environment the Jews as a type of unbelief. It is the pressure of the concrete situation which causes him to make this selection. We may assume that the writer of the Gospel himself may have been of a Jewish heritage, or at least that a large number of those in the local Christian community with him had been Jews. Hence, he is not issuing a judgment upon the Jewish people as a group. He is saying to his original readers that the Jewish opponents of the church are a typical kind of human failure to accept Christ. He represents that kind of rejection with the symbol of the "Jews." And we emphasize that at the hand of the fourth evangelist, the expression, "the Jew," has become a *symbol*.

Hence, the religious significance of the expression, the Jews. This symbol is a part of the broader johannine dualism. Those human beings who fail to see that in Christ there is a fulfillment of the Old Testament heritage—those humans who cling to their pride in themselves—those humans who cannot accept that self-understanding presented in the revelation of God in Christ—these are the persons represented in the symbol, the Jews. They stand on the negative pole of his dualistic scheme as examples of unbelief. They are not an ethnic, geographical, national, or even religious group as much as a stereotype of rejection. *Any person who refuses to accept the human identity proposed by Christ in the gospel is for the evangelist a "Jew."* It may be that the positive pole of the dualistic pair in this case is "Israelite." The Israelite is the one who accepts the revelation (1:31).

A footnote to this all-too-brief a discussion of the use of the expression, the Jews, in the Fourth Gospel may take the form of a question: Why is it that the evangelist is not consistent in his use of the expression? If it is a stylized type that he is using when he refers to the Jews, how can we account for the passages cited early in this section in which the term is not used in that manner? The question may be unanswerable in the final analysis, but there are some possibilities. One is that the evangelist was simply not as consistent a writer as we would like him to be. There are lapses in his stylistic use of the expression. In these cases he (carelessly?) uses the expression in its simple descriptive meaning.

A better explanation is that this inconsistency is a result of the evangelist's use of traditional materials. He had at his disposal stories and sayings which were nurtured in his community before the split from the synagogue came. Back in the days when the Christians were still welcomed participants in the synagogue, narratives and sayings were preserved and developed which used the word Jews in its ordinary meaning. Only when the evangelist drew together his material and wrote the first draft of the Gospel did the stylistic symbol, "the Jews," come into use. This was done after the Christians had been expelled from the synagogue and when the Jews were aggressive in their attacks upon the Christians. As we have suggested above, the evangelist's manner was to preserve traditional material perhaps very often in its original form. He did not alter these older narratives and sayings to make them consistent with his own use of the term, the Jews. Rather he left the word at these points in his Gospel and allowed it to carry its original meaning. Hence, the inconsistent use of the expression. From the modern point of view, our evangelist's editorial work left something to be desired. But as a preserver of the traditions of his community he excelled.

C. JOHANNINE DETERMINISM

Reader's Preparation: The following passages are among those in which something is said concerning the transition from unbelief to belief. Read them carefully and decide for yourself whether or not the Gospel teaches a determinism. That is, do these passages suggest that the evangelist thought only those chosen by God could move from the inauthentic life to authentic existence? Create a list of those features you find in these passages which seem to stress a determinism and those which seem to suggest human freedom. 3:18;21; 3:33-36; 5:24; 6:35-40; 6:44-47; 6:65; 8:47; 10:3-5; 10:14; 10:25-26; 11:25-26; 12:39-48; 17:2; 17:9; 17:12; 17:24; 18:37.

How does one make the transition from the realm of darkness, the world, "the Jews," etc. to the realm of truth, of light, of the above, etc.? How does one move from an inauthentic existence, posited upon the assumption that persons are independent, to an authentic existence which acknowledges creaturehood and dependence upon God? Or, to pose the question in the context of this chapter, how is evil overcome? If evil roots in false human identity, how can that identity be altered? What controls the transition between the two different worlds of John's thought?

These questions lead us into the concept of faith in the Fourth Gospel, and that issue must occupy us fully in the next chapter. But for now we must examine whether or not it is primarily God's pre-determining which effects the destiny of persons or the free will of individuals. Is it free will alone which produces evil, or is it in part the work of God? Again, the Fourth Gospel does not give us a clear answer. There are passages which seem to favor human freedom and those which seem to suggest the dominating will of the Father. Our task will be to lay out the evidence and then explore some possible conclusions.

First, there is considerable deterministic sounding language in the Gospel. Jesus in the Fourth Gospel is made to speak often as if the will of the Father has determined those who would respond to his revelation in Christ. The Father *gives* the Son those who are to believe (6:39; 17:2; 17:6; 17:9; 17:12; 17:24?. This suggests that the first step in the movement from the negative side of johannine dualism to the positive side is the work of God. The Father gives over those who are to believe to the Son. Jesus claims that one must be *drawn* by the Father in order to believe (6:44). Does God "draw" some persons but not others? Belief is not possible unless it is *granted* (6:65). Believing in Christ and hence appropriating true human identity is not simply the work of the individual will. It is an act of God within the individual's life. Some are children of God and others are not. It is only those who are who listen to the truth and embrace it (8:47). The same point is made in a metaphor: Some are sheep of the Good Shepherd and know his voice; others are not (10:3 and 10:26). God seems to make belief impossible for some persons (12:37-40). Some are made deaf to the truth and hence blind to the falsehood of their way of life (8:37).

This kind of language is set over against a clearly implied freedom to believe or not. We need not belabor this theme of the Gospel, for it is somewhat obvious. Believing seems to be up to the will of the individual. Hence, Jesus issues the invitation to believe. "To accept [Christ's] witness is to attest that God speaks true. . . . He who puts his faith in the Son has hold of eternal life, but he who disobeys the Son shall not see that life." (3:33 and 36) We find this language dispersed through the Gospel. How can one *accept,* how can one *obey,* or how can one *put faith* in the revelation unless a person by nature has the capacity to choose freely? A teacher does not offer his class a choice between writing a research paper or a series of book reports if she or he has already decided that every male student shall be required to write a research paper and every female student book reports. The reality of human freedom seems clearly to underlie much of the Gospel.

Here is one of the most puzzling of the contradictions in this enigmatic Gospel. How shall we resolve it? Again, let's explore the possibilities.

1. It could be claimed that one set of passages must be read in the light of the other. Either the deterministic passages are to be taken as the predominant teaching of the Gospel and only qualified by the freedom passages; or the reverse. So, it may be that the point of the Gospel is that *all* persons are selected by the Father for belief. All are given to the Son; all are drawn by the Father; all are granted the capacity for faith. Then it is a matter of individual freedom whether one chooses to accept or reject the God-given capacity to believe. This is a popular and viable way of understanding the evangelist's thought. The opposite understanding is that the deterministic passages are the controlling motif of the evangelist's mind. Only those who are selected by the Father are given the capacity for faith. Others are by divine decision ruled out. Although this position is less popular, it is supportable. The flavor of johannine thought sometimes seems to be that persons are divided into groups—some of whom have a heavenly origin and destiny and some of whom do not. Second century gnostic Christians used the Fourth Gospel upon which to build their speculations that only some humans have that gift to hear and respond to the revelation of truth.

2. Perhaps John intended a contradiction here. Perhaps he intended to say that there is a paradoxical dimension to religious belief. While human choice seems to enter into the acceptance of the truth, the matter is not as simple as that. God has a hand in the matter of the origin of religious faith. One does not believe unless it is divinely granted her or him to do so. But the fourth evangelist—if indeed this was his position—does not attempt to work out the relationship between these two facts. He is not like a modern theologian who might attempt a logical exposition of how divine determination and human freedom are woven together to produce belief. He leaves both assertions side by side in his Gospel with no explanation (much to the frustration of later interpreters like us!). The evangelist may be asserting the fact that there is a mystery about the origin of faith. It is a fact that the reason why some persons are capable of believing and some are not is elusive.

Psychologists of religion probe this puzzle and offer their theories, but the mystery remains. Perhaps you have known a family in which several of the children have developed a genuine religious faith following the example of their parents, but another child has refused to believe. He or she is the religious black sheep of the family. But why? Maybe psychological and sociological—even physiological—data help to understand such a situation. But no explanation seems convincing or certain. The fourth evangelist may have known just such situations in his own community. What he intends to say through his contradictory deterministic and freedom languages is that there is a mystery involved in the human capacity to believe. If this is indeed the answer to the puzzling presence of these opposite motifs in John, then we must credit the evangelist with being sensitive to a peculiarly religious mystery and with being honest enough to say that he had no pat answer for the question.

3. This forces us to face another possibility—an unpopular and unattractive one for most readers of the Gospel. It is that our evangelist was simply not sufficiently astute theologically to see the contradiction he produced in his Gospel. He was not aware that the two sets of passages posed a logical problem. He is naïve enough not to be sensitive to what he was saying. He has produced something like the research paper in which the professor spots a glaring contradiction that had entirely evaded the author of the paper. Between this option for understanding the Gospel and possibility number two we are back to our fork in the road: Either the evangelist is a very profound theologian or else a very naïve one!

4. Finally, we invoke one of our favorite themes in this volume: the suggestion that the evangelist has recorded side by side both his own theological convictions and those of the tradition he is utilizing. Once again he has not tried to reconcile them. He has honored his tradition for its point-of-view, but he has also voiced his own beliefs. Now there is a danger that this kind of distinction between the tradition and the evangelist's own thought could become an easy solution to every contradiction we find in the Gospel. We must beware of using it at every turn of the road. Yet if the orientation of our survey of johannine thought is correct, such an answer remains a possibility. I want for now to leave it at that—just a possibility. I do this because I am not prepared to argue at length that one or the other of the sets of passages we have found is the result of traditional material and the other of the evangelist's thought.

But I will pose a question for your consideration. Could it be that the traditional material the evangelist used originated in a day when the Christians were very optimistic about converting persons to their faith? If so, might not that material have stressed the point that all one must do is decide for the faith? By the time the evangelist wrote, the missionary work of the church had come upon hard days. There were fewer and fewer who were willing to accept the teachings of the church. Especially among the Jews—where the missionary efforts of the Christians has flourished when the traditional material originated—there were drastically fewer converts. So, the evangelist had grown a bit hesitant. His experience led him to think that it took more than an act of will for a person to believe. It took a particular divine gift, a "drawing" of the person by the Father to Christ. Our evangelist was not so bold as to attempt an explanation of the relationship of that divine drawing related to human freedom. He is simply asserting that there seems to be more involved than our fathers and mothers thought back in the "good old days" of the rapid expansion of the church. It is not as simple as, "Believe if you *will*!" There is a sense in which some will never believe, and God must have something to do with that fact.

If this latter option is indeed the case (and we see that it has affinities with elements of some of the other alternatives), the evangelist is quite understandable. It is easy for us to imagine that this kind of change in the situation of the church could have come about. And it is furthermore easy for us to understand how the evangelist could have responded to it the way he did. Back in the 1960s amid the protests against the war in Vietnam, a similar thing happened in America among the anti-war protesters. There was at first a feeling that any sane person, if he or she gave it a moment's thought, would see the senselessness and immorality of the war. But then as the years wore on and those leaders of the protest movement became more seasoned, they lost their optimism. They realized that there was far more at stake for many people in their decision on the war. Economic factors, psychological characteristics, and social affiliations affected the decision whether one would support or oppose the military involvement of the United States in Vietnam. They grew less optimistic about the number of converts their cause would win, but at the same time they grew more realistic and more profound in their analysis of human beings. Such may have been the case in the johannine community. Our evangelist is less optimistic about the freedom of persons to believe the revelation he found in Christ. But he is also more profound in his understanding of the psychology of religious belief. And of course his only explanation was to speak of the hesitancy to believe in terms of God's actions among persons.

D. CONCLUSION

It may appear that we have strayed afield from our original concern for the explanation of evil and from johannine dualism. But not so. The movement from the initial question of the cause of evil to its johannine resolution in a human dualism to the question of freedom versus determinism is inescapable as we try to trace down the outline of the thought of the fourth evangelist. From his insistence upon two different worlds of human self-understanding he must have been led, as we have been, to the question of how one is brought to abandon the way of life which produces evil and take up its opposite. He could not assert his dualism without asking whether or not that dualism was unchangeable. And if it is alterable, how is it altered—by human decision alone or by God's persuasion?

I have argued that for the fourth evangelist evil has its roots in humans.

But more specifically it has its roots in a particular aspect of human life, namely, identity. When persons conceive of themselves as beings who are not dependent upon a creator for their existence, the whole character of existence is thrown out of balance. Because of such a misconstruing of self, the whole of creation is distorted with the result that evil is rampant. Hence, there are two ways of existence open to persons—the way of evil and pretense of independence, and the way of truth and acknowledgment of dependence upon God. These are worlds apart from one another, and they constitute two entirely different worlds. Those two worlds are described in the Gospel both in terms of a human dualism and a cosmic dualism —but the latter is probably simply a way of asserting the enormous importance of the former. The fourth evangelist utilizes a wide spectrum of symbols to describe these two worlds. Moreover, he proposes that the transition from one world to the other is not a simple process dependent entirely upon human choice.

An observation of a sociological nature is appropriate here. John's dualistic response to the reality of evil has roots in his social situation. The church with which he was affiliated had undergone social dislocation. That is, these Christians had been expelled from their original home in the synagogue alongside their Jewish colleagues. This experience must have resulted in a kind of social trauma. Their roots were torn up. They were tossed out into the community stripped of their social alignment with the Jews. Suddenly they had no home. Suddenly they were aliens in the community in which they had come accustomed to live as members of the synagogue. They must have experienced a trauma similar to that known to the Vietnamese refugees who have come to America to escape the rule of the new leaders there. Their whole social orientation is disrupted. The result in the johannine community was perhaps a natural tendency to draw into themselves. They nurtured their own community and group identity. They developed, as it were, an ingroup which looked upon others as an outgroup. This they did both as an effort to reconstruct social identity—to make a new home for themselves in their city—and to defend themselves against the onslaught of their Jewish opponents. Attacked from without, a group always tends to draw in and solidify its unity. (See the provocative article by Wayne Meeks, "The Man from Heaven in Johannine Sectarianism," *Journal of Biblical Literature* 91 [1972], pp. 44-72.)

One of the results of this social reorientation is that a dualistic view of the world developed. The split between the "us" and "them" was natural. Along with it came a tendency to think of themselves as those born from above, as the truth, as the light in a dark world, etc. Similarly, they thought of others who opposed them and their religious faith as born from below, as the world, as darkness, as "the Jews." Dualistic thought satisfied both a theological necessity and a sociological one. Those who are not among us are not only confused about life, they are blind to the truth. They will not believe as we do partly because they have not experienced the divine "drawing" with which we have been gifted.

Now there is an immediate tendency to judge such a course of thought as self-righteous. Nothing is more maddening than a group of persons who believe that they have the truth, and those outside the group are hopelessly lost. But let's not make such a judgment before we have sought understanding. With just a bit of empathy we can understand why the johannine community thought the way it did. We can imagine that we ourselves might have done the same thing if we were in their shoes. Threatened by opponents, socially disrupted, and still in the process of maturing theologically, they understandably found a dualistic distinction between "us" and "them" appealing. The fourth evangelist offered his community a way of understanding what was happening to them. His symbols offered solace and reorientation. His view of evil strengthened the Christians by offering them a way of looking at their situation. What more does religious belief ever do?

A final point with regard to this sociological view of the thought of the fourth evangelist: Theology (or religious thought) is never purely a mental exercise. It is always rooted in the social situation of the believers. We are social animals; and when our social situation shifts radically, we usually shift our religious perspective accordingly. The fourth evangelist and his community are not exceptions to this rule. Johannine dualism is a result of theological minds coming to grips with a social as well as a religious crisis.

The explanation for the reality of evil accepted by the fourth evangelist may or may not be adequate. It may strike you as eminently useful in dealing with the undesirable aspects of life, or it may appear to you as an interesting thesis of a former age which is no longer relevant. It should be obvious to all, however, that our evangelist has taken on a mighty issue and that his thesis concerning evil is only a part of his larger understanding of the meaning of Christ. It is helpful to remember that however he deals with that issue, it may symbolize for us the context of life's tragedy and perplexity in which we hear the Bible's witness to Christ. John's two different worlds are a gallant effort to understand an age-old problem which continues to trouble us.

What we have found is that his dualism trails off into another subject equally important—the nature and origin of religious faith. It is to that subject we must turn. This is properly so, because the religious response to the reality of evil always hinges upon the matter of faith. Whatever a religion teaches with regard to how one deals with evil, it always counsels that its teaching depends upon a faith perspective. You are asked to believe that evil is an illusion, or to believe that it roots in a cosmic being opposed to God, or to believe that it is simply the rhythm of nature. But always you are asked to *believe*. How does one believe? What originates faith? And what after all is meant by faith?

3. Seeing Is Believing— Johannine Concepts of Faith

That old slogan, "seeing is believing," contains a realistic idea: Our belief in anything must have some basis in experience. We ordinarily believe on the basis of that kind of experience which gives reason and motivation for the belief. If someone asserts a point-of-view that seems to be questionable, we naturally ask for some reason to believe that it is true rather than false.

It sometimes seems that those assertions susceptible to scientific inquiry are most easily tested. When a person claims his idea to be true in the sciences, he will often offer us the results of experiments which supposedly demonstrate that the claim is accurate. Similarly, in dealing with everyday needs, we often want some sensory experience before we believe. "The chair will hold you up. Watch me. I'll sit on it." Our experience either enables us to believe or prohibits belief. I watch the television commercial claiming excellent miles per gallon performance by the new automobile. But the new automobile I just bought does not produce such performance. My own experience makes it impossible for me to accept the claims made by the television advertisement.

Likewise, religious affirmations require basis in experience. Religions traditionally make their appeals for belief with the claim that experience offers supportive evidence of one kind or another. This experience is, of course, regarded as much different from that which is usually observed or measured in scientific procedures. Religion claims that internal, emotional kinds of experience lend validity to its ideas and insights. You have heard the testimonies of religious proponents. Peace of mind, satisfaction, serenity, and enrichment are often claimed as the basis of faith. The Zen Buddhist speaks of the great peace and the penetrating insight into experience which results from enlightenment (*satori*). The Christian Scientists testify to a joyful serenity and the release from physical as well as mental pain as a result of their adherence to the teachings of Mary Baker Eddy. Confucians make their case on the basis of the way in which the totality of life makes supreme sense as a result of the practice of their ethic. More primitive forms of religion spoke of the successful experiences in farming, the absence of storms, and the blessed presence of children in their families as evidence that the religious ceremonies were effective. In previous centuries the Calvinists, it is sometimes said, claimed that the truth of their doctrines could be witnessed in the fact that the so-called "elect" were prosperous and wealthy. What more persuasive experience need one have to embrace the faith? More recently the claims of Christianity, in some circles, have been given supposed validation in the experience of success. We hear how Christianity brings peace of mind and success in business, social, and family relationships.

Conversions are often the result of deeply emotional experiences of some sort. John Wesley, the 18th century originator of the Methodist denomination, spoke of the experience of having his heart "strangely warmed." And we have heard claims made for the experiential "proof" of prayer and faith healing. Even the most sophisticated and intellectual forms of Christianity sometimes say that their adherents have basis in experience for their faith. As a result of their beliefs, they claim, their lives are richer and more meaningful, and their relationships deeper.

In general, then, religions assert that there is a positive relationship between faith and experience. Believing originates from an experience or a search for an experience. And continuing belief is founded on the actual experience of living life from a certain faith perspective. Hermann Hesse's famous and intriguing novel, *Siddhartha,* is the story of one man's search for a faith that was supported by his actual experience. While a religion cannot usually make any claim that its position is proven or scientifically verified, it nonetheless suggests that experience points in the direction of the validity of its claims.

The relationship of faith and experience in religion, however, is often rather intricate. It has often been felt that a degree of faith is required *before* we find in our experience the elements which are supportive of belief. In other words, faith is made credible by experience, but before we can understand our experience in a way that it supports faith, we must have faith. One might say then that the very nature of faith is that it is a willingness to trust some claim to truth in expectation that experience will verify that truth. To put it this way, persons must have enough faith to pray once before they have the experience which assures them that their faith is well founded. We might say, then, that there is in religion often a pre-experiential faith and an experiential faith—one which precedes the supportive experience and one which results from the experience. The relationship of faith and experience in religion, then, and especially in Christianity, is a subtle one.

That subtlety is not lost in the New Testament. Everywhere in its pages we find the exploration of the relationship of faith and experience. Paul's letters reflect his personal experiences and their relationship to his growing faith. But nowhere else in the New Testament do we find, I think, the careful and complex treatment of faith and experience that is in the Fourth Gospel. John seems especially concerned with the question of how one is able to affirm Christ without experience and what kind of experience is appropriate to the faithful acceptance of the revelation. In the previous chapter we saw that the evangelist undertook the complexity of the relationship of free choice and divine activity in the origin of faith. That boldness to attack formidable questions continues in the Fourth Gospel as we see the evangelist engage the issue of faith and experience. His task is made difficult by a situation he shares with most of the New Testament writers. The first generation of Christians apparently had some immediate or very close experience of Jesus of Nazareth. Then, the earliest Christians were convinced by some experience which is represented in the Gospels as the resurrection appearances of Christ. Well and good. But what of later generations? What experience leads them to faith? Is it the case that the first generation of Christians stand in a privileged position and none of their descendents had hope of such an experientially based faith? Are Christians after that first group doomed to a "secondhand" experience upon which to build their faith? It is in this context that the evangelist approaches this theme. Writing probably some fifty years after the conclusion of the earthly ministry of Jesus, he must try to understand how experience and faith are related.

Our discussion will deal with a number of interrelated themes:

1. The "signs" as provocators of faith,
2. Seeing and hearing as faith perception,
3. Knowing and believing, and
4. A summary view of faith in the
   Fourth Gospel.

A. THE "SIGNS" AS PROVOCATORS OF FAITH IN THE FOURTH GOSPEL

Reader's Preparation: Study the passages listed below and try to answer two questions: (1) What does the Fourth Gospel mean by the word "sign"? (2) What is the role of the "signs" in initiating and nurturing faith in Christ? 2:1-11; 2:18-25; 4:46-54; 5:1-9; 6:1-28; 9:1-12; 11:1-46; 12:37-41; 20:30-31; 21:1-14. Also read the narrative concerning Thomas in 20:24-29.

What John calls the "signs" performed by Jesus seem to have an ambiguous role in relation to believing in the revelation offered by the Christ of the Gospel. As we seem to find in our explorations of nearly every theme, the Fourth Gospel does not give an easy answer. It is no different in the case of the relation of the experience of signs and faith in Christ.

On the one hand, the signs are works of God, wonders, or expressions of the power of God which produce faith. This is true of each of the seven or eight major signs performed by Christ in the Gospel:

1. Changing the water into wine (2:1-11)
2. Healing the nobleman's son (4:46-54)
3. Healing the man who had been crippled for 38 years (5:1-9)
4. Feeding the multitude (6:1-14?
5. Walking on the water and the miraculous landing (6:15-25)
6. Healing of the man born blind :9:1-8)
7. Raising of Lazarus (11:1-46)
8. Catching a miraculous number of fish (21:1-14).

These are told in such a way as to suggest that they lead to faith. Of the transformation of water into wine it is said, "This deed at Cana-in-Galilee is the first of the signs by which Jesus revealed his glory and led his disciples to believe in him" (2:11). And the signs produce a widespread faith in Christ, we are told in 2:25. Moreover, the evangelist confesses in 20:30-31 that he has reported a few of the many signs Jesus performed in order to provoke faith on the part of the reader.

Furthermore, the implication is that these signs are offered as the evidence that Jesus really is the Messiah (e.g., 2:18). They are his credentials, as it were. They legitimate his claims to that office. Much as one who holds a Ph.D. is expected to legitimate her or his status with learned discussions, so the Messiah is expected to show his identity by performing wonderful deeds. That was, of course, a common Jewish expectation during the first century.

But the evangelist seems to draw a line between believing in Jesus for the sake of his miracles and "seeing signs." What do you make of 6:26? After the feeding of the multitude Jesus again encounters the crowd and says to them, "I know that you have come looking for me because your hunger was satisfied with the loaves you ate, *not because you saw signs*." It appears that what the evangelist means here is that attraction to Jesus in the hope of getting something to eat or of profiting physically or materially in other ways is not the same as following him as a result of seeing the signs he has done. To follow Jesus simply for the sake of his gifts or benefits is not enough. (This would be like following a millionaire and waiting for him to give away five dollar bills.) To do so is not an indication that one really perceives the identity of Christ given expression in the sign. To "see the sign" involves something more than benefiting from this person who can supply your needs. What then is meant by "seeing signs"? Well, this question gets us ahead of our story. But for now it seems that "seeing" the wonderful act of Jesus is more than a visual perception of what Jesus does or the experience of benefiting from those acts. It is an insight into the identity of the performer of the sign. It is grasping that this person is more than a wonder-worker. He is the Christ, the heavenly revealer, the Father's unique Son. Hence, the evangelist has proposed two levels of experiencing the signs of Jesus—a perception of Jesus as a filler of human physical needs and a perception of Jesus as the divine revealer.

In all these cases, the signs are treated in the Fourth Gospel in a very positive way. Even in the last instance in which there is reservation about following Jesus merely for the sake of the benefits of his wondrous works, the signs are still regarded as a positive means of provoking faith in people. But the evangelist elsewhere issues much more serious reservations about the effectiveness of signs in producing genuine faith. He regards them in a positive way in what we have just surveyed, but in a negative way in other passages. First, he recognizes that the signs do not always produce faith. The signs seem impotent to arouse faith in some who experience them (12:37).

This is not a major reservation. But the evangelist goes on. He pictures Jesus speaking in such a way as to cast doubt upon all faith that is grounded in the experience of the signs. Read once again 4:46-53—the healing of the son of the officer in the royal service. Jesus does the healing but only after complaining about belief that is based upon signs and wonderful acts. Is verse 48 of this story a mild rebuke of an excessive dependence upon signs as the basis of faith? Or is it a repudiation of all signs-based faith? Is he saying that faith founded upon wondrous acts has no value at all? Or (a third alternative) are we to infer from these words that faith based upon signs is inferior to a faith that does not require signs? This is a key verse in our examination of the relationship of faith and experience in the Fourth Gospel as it pertains to the signs. Much of what you say on this subject will depend upon your understanding of the words in verse 48.

There are a number of views which can and have been taken. The first is that the faith founded upon signs is a legitimate, mature faith, so long as it is not self-seeking (as mentioned in 6:26). Verse 4:48 is nothing more than a test of the faith of the nobleman. The officer expressed his continuing confidence in Jesus in verse 49. This is similar to the story of the healing of the daughter of the Canaanite woman in Matthew 15:21-28. There Jesus rebukes the woman in response to her request for healing. Her reply to Jesus suggests such profound faith that he immediately effects the healing. The rebuke is not a depreciation of the request for a wondrous deed, but a probing of the degree of faith with which it is made.

The other alternatives are of a different kind. They suggest that this first option does not take account of the fact that a more serious reservation about the role of signs is hinted at in the Gospel. The following three ways of reading the Gospel all propose that the fourth evangelist wanted to revise a view of the signs because he thought that view was improper.

1. Some say that the fourth evangelist wanted to repudiate signs-faith altogether. The signs source which the evangelist used (see the Introduction) contained a very simple theology of the relationship of signs and faith. Signs were wondrous acts which provoke a genuine and adequate faith. The evangelist uses this source, but tries to correct it along the way. He says such signs-faith is not faith at all. It is self-seeking satisfaction. Hence, 6:26 is the evangelist's comment upon that pseudo-faith built upon signs, and 4:48 is a full repudiation of such sign-seeking. If this is so, we have again a situation in which the evangelist has utilized his tradition (in this case the signs source) but tried to correct it. The evangelist's point-of-view would seem to be implied in 20:29 where he commends the kind of faith that blossoms without dependence upon the experience of signs.

2. The position just reviewed is a bit radical. It tries to make too much out of too little in the Gospel. But it does come closer to the truth than the view which sees no reservation in the Gospel about signs faith. A more moderate position is that the evangelist recognizes a faith built upon signs as the first level of faith—the initial stage of faith. But he wants to suggest that such a beginning faith must grow into something more. Faith may begin with a dependence upon signs, but must grow out of that dependence until it matches the faith mentioned in 20:29. This view holds also that the fourth evangelist utilizes a source which holds a more simplistic view of faith. The signs-faith in his source is not repudiated, however, only qualified. He says, in effect, it's alright to build one's faith upon the experience of wondrous works in the beginning. But faith needs to overcome the need for such experiences. It is like the training wheels parents put on their child's first bicycle. It's alright for the child to depend upon those extra little wheels to hold up the bike for a time, but eventually the child must abandon the helper wheels and learn to balance the bike without dependence upon them. Otherwise, as an adult he or she will be out buying training wheels for her or his brand new ten-speed! Let faith depend upon the wondrous works of Jesus for a time! But let it be nurtured until finally those wondrous works are no longer a requirement for Christian belief.

3. The third position is only slightly different. It is that the fourth evangelist did not regard the believing response to the signs as faith but only a preparation for faith. Those who responded affirmatively to the signs of Jesus do not yet believe, but they have an openness to faith that is commendable. Having perceived the wondrous works of Christ, they are ready truly to ''see''—that is, to perceive just who this person is and accept his claims. The reservations about signs-faith in the Fourth Gospel are again the evangelist's revisions of his signs source. Those reservations are simple: Signs-faith is not faith, but it is a valuable first step in the process toward faith. Riding a bike with training wheels is not ''biking,'' but it is a

necessary step for some toward learning the skill of riding a bicycle.

Out of all of this let me propose a view which I think takes account of the evidence we have examined in the Gospel and makes good sense. There are a number of things, I think, which the fourth evangelist is trying to say about signs and their role in provoking faith. First, it is important for us to note that the Gospel recognizes the ambiguity of the signs. Wondrous works are no sure-fire way of producing faith. There is no certain, experiential foundation for faith in Christ, the evangelist is telling us. No matter what roots religious faith has in experience, that experience is never proof of faith. This is so because, as the evangelist apparently knew, experience is always ambiguous. It is always susceptible to numerous interpretations. What one person calls a profoundly religious experience of God, another understands to be the result of certain psychological preconditionings. Our evangelist is no philosopher of religion, but he saw this clearly enough. The most marvelous acts of Jesus are not certainty for faith. They can be understood as acts of one other than the revealer. So he repeats the synoptic testimony that some respond to Jesus and his deeds by asserting not that he was the Christ but that he was possessed by a demon (8:48). The signs of Jesus simply open up the possibilities—either Jesus is one empowered by God in a special way, or else he gains his power from other sources, most likely demonic. In this way, the fourth evangelist continues a biblical view of wondrous deeds, namely, that in themselves they are not absolute proof, but are ambiguous.

Second, in order for signs to contribute in a positive way to the birth and growth of religious faith, they must be perceived in a certain way. They must be seen from a certain perspective which is open to the possibility of God's active involvement in human history. Hence, in order for signs to provoke faith they must be experienced from a perspective which already presupposes faith—at least in a minimal degree. "Seeing signs" then, in the profound sense, is experiencing the acts of Jesus and understanding them correctly. It is seeing through them, as it were, to the true identity of the actor. Insofar as we may call an openness to the possibility of God's reality and activity "faith," the signs *require* faith as well as *provoke* faith. There is an analogy close at hand in the appreciation of art. The viewing of art nurtures one's appreciation for art. Viewing a good painting provokes a new appreciation for artistic expression. But in order to "view" a painting one must already have some presupposed standards for beauty. Unless the viewer holds some conviction about what constitutes beauty, a Picasso is wasted. That pre-condition need not be sophisticated or mature. It may only be an inclination, a vague sense that this is more pleasant to view than that, and so on. But there must be some foundational sense of beauty. So, too, the evangelist seems to be saying that there is a pre-condition for experiencing a sign in such a way that it provokes faith. Whether we call this "faith" or only the first ingredient for faith is irrelevant. What is important is that we see what the evangelist is asserting. "Seeing signs" before faith is impossible. It is like expecting blossoms from the seed before it is even planted.

Our rough little metaphor about the seed moves us to the third point. Seeing signs in this "faith way" begins a process of believing which evolves until the signs themselves are less and less important and the faith perspective all important. I think that we can ascertain just below the surface of the evidence in the Gospel we have surveyed a profound concept of dynamic faith. The experience of grasping the acts of Jesus in a "signful" way requires a kind of embryonic faith. Hence, in the Gospel not all who witness Jesus' acts see them as signs (12:37). That embryonic faith is nourished by the experience of the signs. The evangelist hence affirms the wondrous acts of Jesus as positive experiences for faith (2:23). But that faith does not finally blossom until it no longer needs continual exposure to signs. It becomes a faith that believes without seeing (20:29). We hesitate to oversimplify a matter which the evangelist is trying to show us is a complicated process. But nonetheless we venture a diagram:

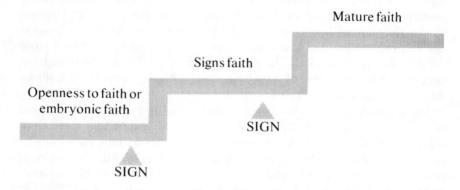

My proposal is then that the evangelist does not depreciate any of these stages in the maturation of faith. But he urges that faith which does not grow beyond its present stage is undesirable. Like the developmental psychologist, he appreciates each stage in maturation but abhors a fixation in any preliminary stage.

It appears to me likely that the evangelist used a signs source which may not have understood either the first or third stages of faith. It did not fully appreciate the reasons for some persons not responding as they should to the wondrous acts of Jesus, nor did it adequately describe how faith must mature beyond its dependence upon signs. That signs source was doubtless a very old collection of narratives having to do with the wondrous works of Jesus, the divine man. The fourth evangelist wants to build upon that understanding and further it. He does so by stressing the ambiguity of the signs and by offering a view of mature faith that needs no signs. He does his revision of the signs source because his generation of Christians had come to know just how unconvincing the recitation of the wondrous works of

Jesus could be. Such a recitation was no longer provoking faith as it perhaps once had. Moreover, the wondrous deeds among the Christians themselves were not as numerous as once seemed to be the case. And so he stresses that his generation of believers ought not to have to depend upon signs in their midst or upon the recitation of signs. They ought to be able to believe without seeing.

One scholar, Robert T. Fortna, proposes that the evangelist made still another revision in the signs source. Fortna discerns in the major signs narratives on two levels. On one level, it is the physical needs of persons that Jesus is made to fill—health, food, etc. On the other level, the physical needs appear as sort of symbols of deeper, spiritual needs. So, while Jesus heals the blind man, the overcoming of blindness is more than a physical healing. In the context of johannine symbolism, blindness suggests darkness, and the healing of blindness, light. Hence, the physical results of the signs are symbols of the deeper spiritual benefits which Christ offers to believers. Fortna is convinced that the signs source which the evangelist used emphasized that Jesus fulfilled these basic physical needs. The evangelist repeats the narratives from his source but wants his readers to appreciate the symbolic meaning they have. So the distinction between following Jesus for the sake of material benefits and seeing his signs (6:26) is the evangelist's signal that these acts of Jesus have important spiritual meaning. Such a proposal makes a great deal of sense and fits neatly into the way in which the evangelist seems to have thought. He and his community are less interested in the sheer material benefits Jesus may have provided his followers than in more spiritual benefits.

Here is a profound understanding of religious faith and its growth. Faith has no ground of absolute certainty. Even the experience of witnessing the historical Jesus offers no certain proof for faith. Faith is a decision to view experience from a peculiar perspective. It is to be open to God's revelation in history, even though our experience is always ambiguous. Moreover, faith is a continuous process of reassessment and growth. But we cannot stop here. The evangelist has much more to say on this subject.

B. SEEING, HEARING, AND BELIEVING IN THE FOURTH GOSPEL

The understanding of faith which we have unearthed in the Gospel in the last section is borne out and further expanded by the evangelist's use of three other terms: seeing, hearing, and knowing. We will examine the first two in this section and leave the last for the next section.

> *Reader's Preparation*: Take a look at the ways in which the words meaning "to see" are used throughout the Gospel. Try to discern some pattern in the evangelist's use of these words. 1:14; 1:50-51; 3:11; 3:32; 5:19; 6:40; 9:39; 14:7; 14:9; 17:24; 19:35-37; 20:8; 20:25; 20:29.

The Greek words for seeing are used in the Fourth Gospel interchangeably for a sensory perception and a faith perception. Examples of the difference between these two are 1:47 and 14:8. In the first it is stated simply that "Jesus saw Nathanael." Here the verb simply means the sensual act of perceiving through the eyes. But in 14:8 Philip asks that Jesus show the disciples the Father. Jesus replies, "Anyone who has seen me has seen the Father." Here the seeing is obviously something more than the mere act of sensory perception. To see the Father in seeing Jesus surely means some sort of spiritual or faith perception. It is to discern in the person of Jesus the nature of the Ultimate Reality. Such a discernment goes beyond the physical sensations of perception. It may be something like that act by which the browser in the art gallery *sees* the Picasso painting but sees also something more. She sees beauty, form, life given expression. Maybe the distinction between physical perception and appreciative perception in the art gallery is parallel to the distinction that the evangelist seems to make between physical perception and faith perception.

John has a profound understanding of the relationship between these two types of perception. This is evident from the manner in which the two types of seeing are connected and even interdependent. 6:40, 11:45, and perhaps 12:45 are good examples of what I mean. In each of these passages, the act of believing follows close upon the act of perception. Perception seems to be an integral part of the process of faith. More specifically, the point is that faith-seeing is based upon the experience of sensory seeing. Perceiving the truth available to the human is a result of perceiving the sheer material, physical object—in this case, the man Jesus. Hence, faith is rooted in sensory experience, but goes beyond the sensory experience to affirm more than the sheer observable data itself will substantiate.

Faith does not blossom out of the inner self entirely. Here the fourth evangelist affirms a basic aspect of the Judeo-Christian tradition. Religious faith is not a result of pure meditation in which one withdraws from the sensory contact with the world into contact alone with one's body. That kind of meditative process may be very good and very helpful. But John, along with the biblical tradition in general, affirms that faith arises from contact with a sensually perceptible object. We might suggest a rough analogy. The young man confidently affirms that the young woman really cares about him because of the way she kissed him. His perception of her care is based upon the physical sensation of the kiss, and we might even say that his understanding of her care *needs* that kiss as a means of communication. But his assertion of her care goes considerably beyond the physical sensation itself. "Ah, it was just a kiss," his friends tease him. But he firmly insists that it meant something more to him. The Christ, John says, affirms the truth of the revelation on the basis of the physical act of seeing Jesus. But that affirmation goes far beyond the physical sensations themselves. The physical or visual observation, with its ordinary interpretations of the data, is needed, but it is only the basis for the further affirmation.

The evangelist's understanding of how experience lends itself to faith is also reflected in other ways in which he uses the verb, to see. His obviously metaphorical use of it in 9:39 makes sense now. Surely, Jesus' mission is to accomplish some healing—vhe bestowal of the physical capacities for sight and hearing—but John means something more. Jesus grants the gift of perceiving the truth about life and existence. He gives the possibility of seeing and hearing so that one may correct their misconstrued self-understanding. That faith perception which is intended with the word ''see'' is also implanted in the assertion that Jesus sees the Father (5:19). Just as the Son sees the Father, so the believer sees (in the sense of faith perception) the Son.

Now much the same thing is true when we turn to the evangelist's use of the words meaning ''to hear'' or ''to listen.''

Reader's Preparation: Now read some of the passages in which the Greek verb meaning ''to hear'' or ''to listen'' is used. What does the evangelist mean by it? 3:32; 5:24-26; 5:30;5:37; 6:45; 6:60; 8:26; 8:40-43; 8:45-47; 10:3; 10:18; 10:26-27; 12:45-47; 15:15; 18:37.

Hearing may be a purely sensory act, as in 6:60 where the words of Jesus are heard but there is no inner perception of their meaning. On the other hand, it may also be the experience from which faith is born (5:24). In the latter case, a discernment of Jesus' true identity begins with normal ''hearing'' but goes beyond it. Failure to believe is rooted in the failure to hear fully and discern the voice of God in the Son. ''The Jews'' cannot believe, for they do not hear properly (8:43).

So faith-hearing, if you will, is the act of discerning the presence of the Ultimate in the voice of this man, Jesus. As with faith-seeing, faith-hearing involves the physical perception and the apprehension of its meaning in a believing way. It is finding a dimension of ultimate meaning in an experience of hearing. Likewise, there is the same parallel between the disciples' hearing the Son and the Son's hearing the Father (8:26). Again, we have evidence that, for the fourth evangelist, the origin of religious faith is in a peculiar discernment of a physical, sensual experience—seeing and hearing.

And so we have in the Gospel of John a two-level experience which is the ground of faith. The base of this experience is the sensual act of seeing the deeds of Jesus and hearing his words.

THE FATHER

The Son sees the Father		The Son hears the Father
THE ACTS OF JESUS		THE WORDS OF JESUS
See the Father	FAITH:	Hear the Father
See Jesus	SENSORY:	Hear Jesus

I hope that you see the similarity between this distinction between sensory seeing-hearing and faith perception and the distinction between the perception of Jesus' marvelous acts and "seeing signs." In both cases, the Gospel presents us with a profound relationship between experience and faith. Faith grows out of an experience which is grasped in a particular way. For John, then, religious faith is a result of our understanding of our experience. One tries to grasp the meaning of what happens to him or her—what is seen, heard, experienced. Faith is the consequent decision to understand experience in a certain way—to see and hear the Father in the acts and words of Jesus. But we are led in a circle back to our previous discussion of determinism and freedom. John recognizes that the seeing and hearing which produce faith already require a certain kind of faith—a willingness to discern the deeper level of reality presented in our experience. If one does not have that willingness, experience cannot give rise to faith. So, the evangelist is driven back to the mysterious dimension of this process. It seems that some are "drawn" to discern that deeper reality, and others are not. That deeper discernment seems to be a gift from God which precedes any faith. The evangelist was not willing to eliminate that aspect of mystery or puzzlement from the process of experience leading to faith. His unwillingness to account for it more fully may seem disappointing to some. Yet it is admirable in some respects; for to us all, it is strange that some persons understand their experience in such a profound way as to be led to religious faith, while others do not.

But we must mention another aspect of johannine thought in this connection. To do so will again get us far ahead of our story, but it seems appropriate here. This understanding of the relationship between experience and faith which we have seen expressed in the johannine treatments of the signs and the verbs to see and to hear is in the profoundest sense *sacramental*. What I mean by this is that John seems to have a deep appreciation for the way sensual experiences lead one to faith. The physical, the sensory, the material is the medium by which faith is born. Now Christian doctrine through the centuries has claimed that to be the case with regard to particular sensory experiences. The water of baptism, the bread and wine of the Lord's Supper—these are physical experiences which nurture faith. As one experiences the sensory, the avenue for grasping the divine is opened up. Now we will argue in chapter four that John has little or no interest in the Christian sacraments. But I will argue there as well that the johannine understanding of faith and experience is fundamentally what the Christians mean by sacramentality. (I mention this now only to help you anticipate the discussion of the sacraments in chapter four.)

John's is a bold assertion when looked at the way we have in the past few pages. The Ultimate Reality of the universe—God—is to be experienced through a grasp of the mundane sensory experiences of life! That is a startling idea. It is particularly so when it is viewed in the context of other religious traditions of the world. Seeing and hearing are the necessary prerequisites for believing. We must not minimize John's position by assuming that he meant it only in the context of a particular historical person, Jesus. That is, I think John does not mean that faith was born among the first disciples by the sensual act of seeing and hearing Jesus of Nazareth, but, after the departure of the man Jesus, it is no longer the same. I think that he is more concerned with his readers in the 80s and 90s than that. He is saying that the first disciples saw and heard the historical Jesus and their faith grew out of such physical experiences. But I think he means too that every Christian's faith is born out of sensual experiences of seeing and hearing. The Christ of faith is still to be seen and heard in the community of believers. From the hearing of Christian preaching and witness and from the seeing of acts done in Christian love, faith is still born. So, his *sensory theology* is right for his own day, not just for the era of the life of Jesus of Nazareth.

John's solution to the question of experience and faith is an interesting and even daring one. But there is another matter which has crept into the focus of our attention, namely, the relationship of knowing and believing.

C. KNOWING AND BELIEVING IN THE FOURTH GOSPEL

The discussion of the relationship between faith and knowledge is a classic issue in Christian circles. Scholars have fought over the subtleties of the relationship for centuries. Is there a requisite knowledge which one must have before faith? Or, is faith the foundation for knowing? The history of the discussion in Christian circles cannot concern us here, nor do we want to pose the johannine treatment of these themes necessarily as the answer to the theologians' problems. We do want to note, however, that as early as the first century of the Christian movement there was a man whose way of thinking encompassed a relationship between faith and knowledge. It is that which we want to examine now.

> *Reader's Preparation:* The necessary reading for our brief discussion of this subject will be satisfied by the following passages: 6:69; 8:31-32; 17:7-8; 21-23. But as you read these three passages, ask yourself: Which comes first in the johannine scheme—knowing or believing? Is one more important than the other? Are they synonyms?

Do persons know something they did not previously know after they believe something to be true? More simply, is there knowledge arising from belief? Or, must one first have some knowledge before one believes? Listen to the fourth evangelist: In 8:31 it sounds like those who believe in Christ then, as a consequent, know something. (10:38 seems to make the same point.) But wait! 17:8 suggests the opposite. The disciples know that Christ came from the Father, and therefore (or shouldn't we supply a "therefore" between the sentences?) they believe. (See also 16:30 where the same relationship may be meant). In the first case,

$$\text{faith} \longrightarrow \text{knowledge}$$

In the second case,

$$\text{knowledge} \longrightarrow \text{faith}$$

But a simple contradiction like this is not enough in our puzzling Gospel. There must be a still further confusing factor. In some passages it sounds as if the Greek words for knowing and believing are used synonymously. "We have faith, and we know," confesses Peter (6:69). And in 14:7 and 17:3 it appears we could substitute the word "believe" for the word "know" and have exactly the same meaning. In these cases then,

$$\text{faith} = \text{knowing.}$$

Now there are scholars who would have us make fine distinctions between faith and knowing in the Fourth Gospel. They find a more intellectual sense in those passages where knowing is used and a more volitional one where believing is used. Bultmann wants us to believe that knowing in the Fourth Gospel refers to the "structural" quality of believing (*Theology of the New Testament,* vol. II). It seems to me, however, that such arguments are straining the evidence. They are trying to get philosophical distinctions out of the text which are simply not there. The johannine view is simpler than that!

The reason John can use faith and knowing interchangeably is that they are really synonymous in his mind. What he means by "to know" is no different from what he means by "to believe." So the key to the relationship of these two in the Fourth Gospel is those passages in which we sense that we can substitute one word for the other without distortion of meaning. John was not a philosopher. He was not concerned with epistemology. But that does not mean that his equation of these two was done thoughtlessly.

John can use knowing as a synonym for believing, I think, because he uses the former word in its Hebraic sense. Even though he is writing in Greek, his Jewish background leads him to think of knowledge in a Hebraic way. In the Old Testament the Hebrew word for "knowing" had less of a sense of cognitive or intellectual comprehension than it did in the Greek language. Knowing refers in the Old Testament to a personal relationship. It is not a detached apprehension of an object. When we say in our language that we know something, as a book, it means that we have examined it, studied it. We can describe it to you as an object.

The Old Testament confuses us then when it says that so and so went in and "knew" his wife and she conceived a son. What does it mean that he *knew* her? Obviously it means something other than objective, detached observation. The Hebrew word, *yadah*, which we most readily translate "to know" means to enter into personal, intimate relationship. It is subject and subject in a relationship of mutual involvement. Hence it is used of sexual relationship in much the same way that we might say that a couple has "intercourse"—two subjects in a relationship of trustful interchange. Similarly when the prophet Hosea says that his people suffer from a lack of knowledge of God (4:6f), he is not complaining that their theology is faulty. He is saying rather that their personal relationship with Yahew is dead.

When John employs the Greek word, *gnōskein*, he means it in its profound Hebraic sense. As a subject one has entered into a personal and trusting relationship with another subject. He could then use it as a synonym for belief, for it suggested the same kind of relationship which exists in faith. He does not, I think, intend by its use to say that there is some greater degree of intellectual content or exchange when he uses "know" than when he uses "believe." Both are personal. Both are intimate. Both are subject to subject, not subject to object. There is no detachment, but just the opposite—involvement.

This tells us one thing about the johannine concept of faith. If John means what we think he means by knowing and if he can use that word as a synonym for faith, then what he means by faith begins to come clear. Faith is the trusting personal relationship between two subjects. It is an interchange on a most intimate level between two beings of personal nature. Belief must not then mean merely the intellectual acceptance of doctrine (although there is some of that in the Fourth Gospel, as we will soon see). It must mean that faith involves the whole person—mind, body, emotions, and all the rest—in a personal relationship.

The story is told of the man who was going to walk a tightrope across Niagara Falls pushing a wheelbarrow in front of him. The crowd gathered on the day for the risky endeavor. The wind was blowing mightily. It whipped the rope back and forth. As the time for the walk grew close, the crowd began calling out its advice: "Don't try it! You'll never make it!" Then one man jumped from the crowd and approached the tightrope walker. He said to the adventurer, "Go ahead! Make the walk. You can do it! I have faith in you." To this encouragement the tightrope walker replied with an invitation: "Okay, if you believe in me so strongly, you get in the wheelbarrow and come with me!"

Johannine faith is not a detached intellectual confidence. It is a personal involvement and trust which links the believer and the object of belief into a kind of unity. That relationship of faith was such that our evangelist could describe it in the Hebraic sense of knowing. Yet this insight is still something of an overgeneralization. We can qualify what we have said about the concept of faith in the Fourth Gospel in several very important ways.

D. SUMMARY VIEW OF FAITH IN THE FOURTH GOSPEL

> *Reader's Preparation:* Skim through the gospel one more time. Make a
> list of the answers the Gospel gives to the following questions: (1) What is
> the object of belief? (That is, what are the people asked to believe?) (2)
> What is the nature of belief as it is used in the Gospel?

Ninety-eight times the Gospel uses the verb, to believe *(pisteuein)*.
Believe! But what is it that I am asked to believe? There are at least three
different objects of faith for the Fourth Gospel. That is, what one is asked to
believe or believe in varies:

1. Most often the point seems to be a personal allegiance to Jesus, a
personal relationship with him. This occurs for example in 4:39. And so the
most common construction is the use of the verb "believe" with the
preposition *eis* (into or in), and the object of the preposition is most often
Jesus himself. This object of the verb suggests that our proposals about the
nature of faith at the conclusion of the previous section are prominent in the
Gospel.

2. But sometimes the object of the belief is not the person but the
statements he makes. "Believe the words Jesus speaks." (e.g., 2:22) This
is not substantially different from the first object of faith, Jesus himself,
except here faith is a credence in the statements of the revealer rather than
faith in the person of the revealer. John is likely implying that the one
involves the other. If you put your faith in Jesus as the revelation of God,
you believe what he says to be true.

3. A different thing is suggested, however, by the third object of faith.
Sometimes it is faith in statements *about* Jesus. Now the reader is not asked
to believe in the person of Jesus in the sense of a personal relationship of
trust. Nor is the reader asked to take as true what Jesus says. The reader is,
instead, called to believe that Jesus is the revealer, the Messiah, the
Father's Son (e.g., 11:27). This use of the word "believe" has shifted the
meaning of faith from a personal relationship to an intellectual acceptance.
My faith is a faith in a creed, in this case, not in a person.

The fourth evangelist has presented us then with two different kinds of
faith in Christ. The first is a personal involvement with and allegiance to
Jesus. This involves personal trust and intimacy. The second is an understanding of faith as acceptance of a creed, or at least of creedal assertions
about Christ. The former is the older form of Christian faith; the Pauline
concept of faith is essentially of this kind. The second is the kind of faith
which we witness emerging only later in the New Testament period. It is
like the use of the word "faith" in some of the very latest New Testament
literature. There faith has been transformed into creed or doctrine. "The
faith" is not a dynamic personal relationship between the Christian and
Christ, but a set of doctrinal statements about Christ. (See for example,
James 2:17; Hebrews 11; Jude 3; 1 John 5:1; and 3 John 4-11.) This change is

an important one. It utterly transforms the nature of believing. It moves it into an area which can be reduced to a mere intellectual matter. The first meaning of faith had a far more personal dimension and demanded the whole of the believer's person. It would be like first loving another person, then coming to love the statements you could make about that person. To love the affirmation, "She is a really caring individual," is radically different from loving the person herself.

Now, our evangelist appears to be partly responsible for the beginning of the gradual shift in the early church toward a creedal understanding of faith. Of the literature in which we can find statements using the word "faith" with a creedal ring about it, the Fourth Gospel is probably the earliest. Here I want to say that the fourth evangelist was not aware of the shift in usage he was making. His fundamental sense of faith is the personal relationship. But his community is under attack. They are suffering social dislocation and are in the midst of an identity crisis. What clearly separates them from their opponents is that they can make certain affirmations about Christ. This fact is important, for it structures a sense of identity and group solidarity. "We are the ones who can affirm that Jesus is the Messiah." That functional value of the creedal nature of the faith concept seduces the evangelist into its use. He does not see it as a violation of his other fundamental concept of faith—a personal relationship with Christ. And, of course, he is unaware of how the personal dynamic character of faith could be submerged beneath an emphasis upon the creedal character. Regardless of his motivation, we must credit (or blame) the fourth evangelist for an early reduction of faith to creed. Whether that was a tragic move or only the logical conclusion of his other view of faith, I leave to your own judgment.

But we must conclude this section on a more positive note, having saved the best for last. There is still one other feature of the johannine concepts of faith which we have not mentioned. It begins with a grammatical observation. The fourth evangelist never uses the noun, faith or belief, but always and only the verb, to believe. (We must mention here that the Greek has only one word which we must translate variously belief or faith.) What does this mean? That he liked verbs rather than nouns? It means of course that for him belief is always an active matter. Faith is not an inner disposition. Faith is not something one *has*. Faith is something one *does*. Faith is not a static being but a dynamic becoming. If faith is always a verb, that surely implies that faith is not something one does once and is unnecessary thereafter. Rather, faith as a verb means that believing is a decision made once only to have to be made over and over again. Faith is a continuing dynamic. It is not a state of being.

Now this understanding of faith implicit in the use of the verb instead of the noun indicates that the evangelist's fundamental concept of faith is that of personal relationship. While he uses the verb, to believe, in conjunction with creedal statements, that is not the primary thrust of his Gospel. It is rather a digression, a lapse—and a very important one at that. But basically the Fourth Gospel affirms that out of experience comes a trusting relationship with a personal being.

E. CONCLUSION

Our evangelist is not a philosopher of religion. His exposition of the relationship of faith and experience is done within the context of a gospel. And a gospel is not a philosophical or even a theological treatise. It is rather a document designed to preserve traditional material and address that material in a newly relevant way to the issues confronting a community of faith. The concern of the fourth evangelist is to nurture religious faith in the midst of severe trials and difficulties. It is, therefore, unreasonable to expect of his work a logically consistent and complete exposition of the question of the relationship of faith and experience. The philosopher does not read social protest literature for its rational explication of philosophical issues. On the other hand, implicit in a social protest are certain views— basis values, understandings of society, of person, and of freedom. So, too, we must not read the Fourth Gospel expecting philosophical dissertations on issues such as faith and experience. Still, we find in the Fourth Gospel a view of that relationship which has been expressed in order that the evangelist might accomplish his major goal, namely, the nurturing of faith.

What we find then in the Fourth Gospel is a rather profound view of the way in which religious faith is rooted in experience. It is a relatively bold view of the matter, for it affirms the positive role of sensual experience in the origin of faith. It assigns a primary place to the perception of signs and the basic experiences of sensory perception such as seeing and hearing. But it claims that beyond that sensory perception must come a deeper, or extra-sensual perception. If this exists within the consciousness of a person, then out of experience may be born a personal relationship of trust with the Divine Person. That relationship may be variously described as faith or knowledge (in its Hebraic meaning). And from that basic relationship, faith may sometimes be understood as the acceptance of creedal statements.

But when we probe beneath what the evangelist means by this kind of faith-perception of the words and deeds of Jesus we are confronted with unresolved mystery. He leaves us no clear explanation for the initial openness to the deeper discernment which produces faith. His dynamic view of faith, which must grow and mature, begins in a mystery. We may conclude that the evangelist does not adequately break a circle of thought which begins with that willingness to see divine activity in the midst of personal experience and ends in mature faith. To put it differently, faith is required for experience to give birth to faith! We are left with the feeling that the divine participation in the individual surely begins with the individual's effort to understand experience. But the evangelist does not seem willing to assert this fully and thus violate the role of human freedom in the origin of faith. We view his thought in its best light when we summarize the view of faith and experience in the Fourth Gospel this way: God grants all persons the capacity to perceive the depth dimension of their experience, the dimension in which divine reality resides. But each individual is left with the freedom to use or not use that capacity. And if they do avail themselves of it, they are then able by the faith-perception of their experience to come into a personal relationship with the divine reality. That relationship in turn may grow beyond the dependence upon the sensual dimension of experience. But such a growth depends upon the constant nurturing of faith.

Our evangelist has not settled once and for all the question of experience and faith. His contribution on this score may seem insignificant in the context of the world's religious traditions. For it is only one among many. But I suggest that his view is at least one of the most creative answers to this question one can find early in a religious tradition. Without benefit of centuries of discussion and without benefit of vast philosophical categories and refinements, his is a responsible and personal interpretation of faith. It most certainly merits our study and our criticism in the light of the Christian tradition's ongoing reflection on the meaning of faith.

So, the evangelist explores the meaning of faith and its origin in experience with considerable skill. Faith represents for him the way in which the individual passes from one pole of the human dualism to the other. It is the means of transition between darkness and light, death and life, and falsehood and truth. But what is the character of this light, this life, and this truth? What is the accomplishment of faith? What has one gained by believing? This leads us to the final major segment of our survey of johannine thought. It leads us to his concept of the life of the believer.

4. Eternity Is Now—
   Johannine Eschatology

During the presidency of Richard Nixon, a cartoon appeared which suggests in an indirect way the theme of this chapter. The scene is in front of the White House. One bearded and rather weird looking fellow wearing a long robe is carrying a sign which declares, "The End is Near!" He is looking in surprise at another figure whose back alone we can see. The second figure is, however, recognizable as the current resident of the White House, and he is carrying a sign which states, "Four More Years!" This blending of religious and political motifs suggests the tension between the present and the future. It epitomizes in the religious figure those who believe that the present is the time of fulfillment and in the political figure those who look expectantly to the future for fulfillment.

This theme of the tension between the future and the present as the time of fulfillment is another of the classical religious questions. All religions teach in one form or another the hope that human fulfillment and satisfaction is available. This teaching is often expressed in the concept of salvation. It declares that human beings may achieve that for which they were intended from their creation. It declares that the deepest longings of the human soul may be fulfilled, that basic needs may be met, and that hopes may be realized. Such a promise of salvation, however, may be in the distant future, or it may be promised in the believer's present time. In some religious traditions, the fullness of salvation is promised only in the future (for instance, in a heavenly home after death). There will come a time, these religions teach, when humanity will be perfected, but that time lies in the future. Christianity and Judaism both seem generally to fit into this category. In other religious traditions, the fulfillment of the promised salvation is available immediately. The Zen Buddhist master hopes subtly to lead his students to that experience of enlightenment which is the actualization of the serenity for which humans were intended.

But, of course, the distinction is never this sharp. Although the Christian tradition generally teaches a future fulfillment, one often finds the declaration of the anticipation of that future fulfillment in the believer's present. The experience of the Holy Spirit is often understood in this way. Indeed, the Apostle Paul spoke of the Spirit as a sort of downpayment on the future fulfillment promised by God. The experience of the Spirit is a guarantee that there shall be a completion of salvation (e.g., Romans 8:23). Among those Christians of a mystical bent, one finds a declaration that the Christian is able in this life to experience nearly the fullness of God's promised salvation. Similarly in the Eastern religions, the promised goal is often the unity with God in the state of Brahman or Nirvana. That state comes to the most faithful upon their death and ends the cycle of endless life (especially Hinduism). Still, one experiences something of this final state in this life as a result of meditation. So, it is obvious that religions blend the ideas of the future and present fulfillment of the promised salvation.

Therein lies the issue at stake in this chapter. Is the salvation promised to the believer a future possibility alone? Or, is it to be found in the believer's present experience? Or is it the case that the present is in some way a partial fulfillment which anticipates the completed fulfillment in the future? While generalities break down, there is a degree of truth in the assertion that some religious teaching about salvation is future oriented, some present oriented. In the former case, it is hope that plays a primary role. Hope for the future consummation of God's plan. In the case of those who are present oriented, the emphasis shifts. The hope can be realized now. It is being realized. Live for the now! Inherent in this question is a basic struggle of religions to resolve the present experience of the believer and her or his future hope.

Christianity was probably born amid a belief that the salvation of humanity lay in the future, and that the future was very near. Earliest Christianity was bred amid the fervent hopes of Judaism for the imminent appearance of the Messiah and the age he would inaugurate. Christianity in this regard was not far different from those Jews responsible for the Dead Sea Scroll literature. In their community at Qumran on the Dead Sea, these Jewish fanatics prepared themselves for the impending appearance of the Messiah and the great battle with evil which would ensue. Earliest Christianity was nurtured on this kind of Jewish apocalypticism. Some of the earliest literature from the Christian movement stresses just this point, for example, 1 Thessalonians.

But the Christians very quickly also came to believe that there was an experience of divine fulfillment to be had in the present time. The believer experienced the presence of the living Christ and was given gifts which were anticipations of the final gift of full salvation. Paul, for instance, speaks of salvation both as a present experience and a future hope. This is clearest in his declaration in Romans 8:24: "For we have been saved, though only in hope." Many critics of the New Testament contend that the early Christians had to struggle with the disappointment resulting from the delay of the return of Christ. First, it was believed that Christ would very soon return (the "parousia," as it is technically called in the New Testament). With his return he would bring the fullness of God's salvation. But that immediate reappearance did not materialize. When it did not and the hope for Christ's return was pushed further into the future, more attention was focused upon the sense in which salvation was already present in the believer's life.

Into this drama of the development of early Christian belief comes the Fourth Gospel. Its place in that unfolding struggle between future hope and present realization is significant. In few other pieces of religious literature (at least Christian literature) is the tension between the present and future dimensions of salvation more evident. Scholarly debate wages over the position of the fourth evangelist on this question. But all must agree that there is a remarkably strong emphasis in the Gospel upon the presence of salvation in the believer's life. Perhaps no other New Testament document stresses more strongly than the Fourth Gospel the realized hopes of Christians. That motif of the presence of salvation comes to expression in the Fourth Gospel in a number of ways. First, of course, it is present in the way in which the evangelist deals with eschatological themes. (Eschatology is simply a handy word to summarize those beliefs in what will occur at the "last day"—at the end of time—in Christian thought.) But the presence of salvation is also stressed in the way in which our evangelist handles a number of other topics, especially the Spirit, the church, and the sacraments. What ties together the themes which we will be discussing in this chapter is the single idea which the evangelist held: Salvation is already accessible to the believer in this time. Or, to summarize the idea less prosaically, eternity is *now*!

The following pages will treat in turn, then, these matters:

1. The evangelist's view of the fulfillment of promises related to the final time (i.e., eschatology),
2. His view of the presence of the Spirit among believers (pneumatology),
3. His view of the community of Christian believers (the church or ecclesiology), and
4. His view of the sacraments (sacramentality).

It is the thesis of this chapter that what the evangelist says through each of these subjects is that the promised salvation is already available. Hence, his views of the Spirit, the church, and the sacraments are intertwined with his understanding of eschatology. He believes the promises related to the final time are already fulfilled in the lives of believers. That belief is expressed in his views of the Spirit, the church, and the sacraments, as well as eschatology.

A. JOHANNINE ESCHATOLOGY

I have already mentioned that critics of the Fourth Gospel are divided on the question of the relationship of the present experience of and the future hope for salvation. This is so because the evidence of the Gospel is not clear. Our first task in this section is to try to get before us the relevant passages. In some the evangelist seems to affirm that the full salvation of the individual lies in a future day. In others he seems to declare that those hopes for the future are already realities in the believers' lives.

> *Reader's Preparation:* Below are the most important passages having to do with eschatological hope. Read them carefully and try to determine whether the evangelist is talking about the fulfillment of these hopes in the future or in the present. 3:18-19; 3:36; 5:21-29; 6:39-54; 9:39; 11:23-25; 12:25; 12:31; 12:48; 14:2-3; 14:18; 14:28; 17:1-26. Read chapters 15 and 16 and note what is said there about the tribulations the believers will face or are facing.

By now you have grown accustomed to contradictions in the Gospel. So, you are not surprised to find contradictory statements on this issue. But here the contradictions seem more pronounced and more important. We propose the following as a brief summary of the problem of johannine eschatology. You may want to challenge some of it or add to it in the light of your reading of the evidence.

PRESENT REALITIES	FUTURE REALITIES
Judgment (e.g., 3:18; 9:39)	Judgment (e.g., 12:48)
Eternal Life (e.g., 3:36; 5:24)	Eternal Life (e.g., 12:25)
Resurrection (e.g., 5:21; 5:24; 5:26)	Resurrection (e.g., 6:39-40; 6:54)
	Parousia (e.g., 14:3; 14:18; 14:28)
	Tribulations which signal the advent of the Messiah (chapters 15 and 16)
Defeat of the "ruler of this age" (12:31)	

It is understandable if we get frustrated at some point in studying the evidence, for there seem to be no less than three kinds of eschatology in the Fourth Gospel. The *first* we will call "futuristic eschatology," because it seems to hold that the promised salvation is in the future. Judgment will come at the future last day of history (12:48). There will be a resurrection of the dead on that decisive day (6:39-40 and 6:54). The future resurrection and judgment are associated with one another (5:28). To this add the fact that John seems to look for a future coming again of Christ (chapter 14).

Further supplement it with the references in chapters 15 and 16 to the tribulations to be experienced by the Christians. We should point out that a standard idea in the futuristic eschatology of early Christianity and first century Judaism was that of the tribulations which occur as the last day approaches. Just before the appearance of the Messiah (in Jewish thought) or the second appearance of Christ (in Christian thought) evil would abound. Hence the believers would be severely persecuted. The references to the tribulations in chapters 15 and 16 of the Fourth Gospel seem to have the sound of those "messianic tribulations." It appears that John accepted the idea that just before things become a whole lot better they are going to get very much worse.

Now these futuristic expectations fit with the traditional early Christian view of eschatology. They express the idea that history would be brought to a grand conclusion. Christ would reappear, this time triumphantly. Evil would be defeated and Satan's rule ended. There would be a mass resurrection of the dead followed by a judgment. Some of those judged would be given eternal life. Nothing in all of this surprises the experienced student of the New Testament who has had an opportunity to explore the culture of the first Christian century. These concepts have roots in the early Christian adaption of Jewish apocalyptic thought. We find similar ideas not only in other New Testament writings, but in Jewish writings of the two centuries before the Christian era as well as the first century itself. These passages affirm a historical dualism. The present age is ruled by Satan, and it will end to be followed by the eternal age ruled by God alone.

But there is a *second* kind of eschatology in the Gospel which we will call "present eschatology." This is found in those passages in which John seems to say that the future expectations of the Christians are already realized now in their relationship with Christ. One is already judged by his or her response to Christ (e.g., 3:18). Resurrection is the experience of being brought to a new understanding of oneself by belief in Christ. One is brought from death to life in the immediate present by faith (e.g., 5:24). The story of the resurrection of Lazarus is instructive here. Mary meets Jesus after he has finally come to the village where his friend Lazarus has died. Jesus says to Mary, "Your brother will rise again." Mary sounds like she is reciting the proper words of traditional Christian belief: "I know that he will rise again at the resurrection on the last day." One cannot help but feel that the words are slightly impersonal or rhetorical. Mary says them, but conviction is lacking. Rather, she says them but they do not seem to help much in the face of her brother's death. Jesus then answers her with one of the "I am" sayings: "I am the resurrection and I am life. If a man has faith in me, even though he die, he shall come to life; and no one who is alive and has faith shall ever die." Then Jesus goes about restoring Lazarus to life. The point of the chapter seems to be that a faith relationship with Christ is resurrection. Resurrection is not some vague hope for something that will happen way out there in the shadowy future. It is a present experience when Christ is present.

More present eschatology is expressed in the assertions concerning eternal life. To live with faith in Christ is already to live eternal life (5:24). The expression eternal life is, of course, part of that johannine dualism we have discussed. It seems to mean the quality of existence of the believer. It is not a future hope (but let's not forget 12:25). It is a present reality accruing from the faith acceptance of Christ. It is, if you will, the new self-understanding which results from accepting the revelation of God in Christ. To be sure, it may have something to do with survival of physical death (as chapter 11 affirms), but it is primarily a quality of life. We might say that it is the quality of life which results from a proper self-understanding which cannot be annihilated by death.

This kind of eschatology is new. It has affinities with some of the things Paul says about the presence of salvation in the believer's experience. But it is a radical assertion that the future hope is *now*. John has taken those experiences connected with the last day in traditional Christian eschatology and declared, "They are present now in the believer's life!" He has reversed the direction of Christian expectation, at least in these passages. He has turned that expectation away from the future and toward the present. This present eschatology of his is different. It is new and fresh in early Christian thought, we think. But before we explore this any further, we must look at the *third* kind of eschatology and then try to reconcile the conflict among the three.

A "heavenly eschatology" is given expression in some of the later chapters of the Gospel. This is an eschatology which is futuristic, but it is quite different from traditional futuristic eschatology in early Christian thought. There is a heavenly home waiting for the Christians. Christ will take them there (14:2-3). In that heavenly place apparently there will be a perfecting of the relationship among the Christians and between the Christians and God. They will attain a perfect oneness (17:23). Now this heavenly eschatology is not explicitly associated with the futuristic eschatology. That is, it is not stated that following the resurrection and judgment Christians will be taken to their heavenly home and perfected. It sounds more as if it is something that occurs after the death of the individual Christians, and this heavenly perfection is simultaneous with the continuance of world history. If this is the case, then we have still another radically different view of the promise of salvation. It is not a part of a historical dualism like the futuristic eschatology of the gospel seems to be. Rather, it suggests a cosmic dualism. There are two realms in the cosmos —the world and heaven. In the heavenly realm Christians have a place, and there they are promised perfection. (Ernst Käsemann is the one who has most recently brought this heavenly eschatology to light.)

How can we come to terms with the presence of these three different forms of eschatological thought in the same Gospel? Another contradiction in the Gospel cries out for resolution. Again, let me suggest some alternatives before I present my way of solving the conflict among these three.

1. The "both and" solution is first. It simply affirms that John means all he says. The "heavenly eschatology" is not to be disassociated from the futuristic one. It is part of what the believer may hope for in the future consummation of God's plan. The evangelist simply neglects to make that association explicit. There is no cosmic dualism in the heavenly eschatology. The heaven is simply the new age that dawns with the completion of God's work in Christ. So the events of the heavenly eschatology are to be understood as a further historical sequence of the futuristic eschatological events. Moreover, the split between the future and present eschatologies is not to be exaggerated. Like Paul, all the evangelist means is that the future blessings of the Christian are already beginning to be available in their relationship with Christ. To have eternal life and resurrection now is simply to have the promise of them. The fulfillment of these blessings still resides in the future. The present holds the taste of the future. It is the down payment and the future will bring the full payment. The hors d'oeuvres enable the diner to anticipate the tasty meal that will be coming soon. So, the present eschatology of the fourth evangelist means to say that these experiences are a foretaste of things to come.

This view of the eschatology of the Gospel makes the evangelist look rather orthodox. Perhaps he does stress the present a bit more than the future, but he does not stress it to the elimination of the future hope. This alternative would have us take everything the evangelist says with equal seriousness and see that he relates it all in a traditional way.

2. The "spoiler" alternative is quite different. It is the thesis of some (most adamantly, Rudolf Bultmann) that John himself wrote only the present eschatalogy passages. The evangelist entirely rejected the future eschatology and believed only in the fulfillment of the promises in the present. Bultmann understands that the evangelist "demythologized" the futuristic eschatology. That is, he understood all of the symbolism about the resurrection at the last day, etc., in terms of the possibilities of the present relationship with the Father. When the evangelist finished his Gospel there was no futuristic eschatology at all to be found in its pages.

But then along came a "spoiler." A rather orthodox believing Christian got hold of the Gospel. He did not like all that he read there. So, he took it upon himself to "repair" the Gospel. Among other things, what he did was to supply the Gospel with a futuristic eschatology. It is he who wrote the passages which stress that the promises are yet to be fulfilled. Bultmann argues that this churchly reviser of the Gospel left evidence of his work. His work can be separated out by means of an analysis of style and content, as well as the way in which his work causes breaks in the flow of the narrative.

The "spoiler" alternative can also account for the heavenly eschatology in several different ways: First, some argue it is part of the evangelist's own present eschatology. The believers are in their Father's house in the community of believers. It is there they are perfected into oneness. Hence the heavenly eschatology is reduced to a part of the evangelist's present eschatology. But, second, Bultmann went on to say that the evangelist maintained that the quality of the believer's present existence would survive the grave. So, the evangelist did believe in a life beyond death which would continue the faith existence once begun in this life. In this way the heavenly eschatology is harmonized with the present eschatology as a part of the work of the evangelist. Only the futuristic eschatology is the work of the reviser of the Gospel, who in effect spoiled the harmony of the Gospel's position on this question.

3. The "preserver" alternative is different in only one way. Bultmann is correct in saying that the evangelist in his present eschatology is reinterpreting (demythologizing) futuristic eschatology. But this alternative proposes that the futuristic passages came to the evangelist in his tradition and are preserved by him in the Gospel. Rather than arguing that a "spoiler" added the futuristic eschatology, this solution claims that that view of eschatology is there as a result of the evangelist's concern to preserve traditional materials. As he did in other aspects of his tradition, the evangelist incorporated traditional eschatological materials even though they contradicted his own theological stance. He respected the tradition and honored its place among the members of his community. But he also added his own eschatology—the present and heavenly themes.

In a sense, what he was trying to do was to take the symbols of the older futuristic eschatology and express their meaning for Christians of his day. That he did this is evidenced by the proximity of the futuristic and present passages to each other in the test of the Gospel. Perhaps you noted how often the present and future eschatologies are found in the same chapter together, e.g., 5:24-26 and 5:27-30. Often (but not always) the evangelist repeats the traditional symbols of the futuristic eschatology near the point at which he has offered the new interpretation of them in present eschatology. The contradictions are in his Gospel because he is such a faithful preserver of tradition.

This alternative would agree with Bultmann that the evangelist held to a heavenly eschatology which was consistent with his present eschatology. Or, it might argue that heavenly eschatology is intended only as a symbolic expression of the present eschatology. It might be that the cosmic dualism of the heavenly eschatology means only that the present life of the believer is the meeting of the divine and human realms. We suggested in the chapter on johannine dualism that the evangelist's cosmic dualism might be a symbolic articulation of his human dualism. It might be argued too that his heavenly eschatology is a more poetic way of expressing those beliefs having to do with present eschatology.

We believe that the "preserver" solution to the contradictions in johannine eschatology is the most promising of the three alternatives. Our study has found consistently that the evangelist preserved traditional material even when it contradicted his own view of matters. We found, too, that he often attempts an interpretation of the traditional materials for his own day (e.g., the understanding of faith in the signs source). Therefore, it seems entirely possible that what we have in johannine eschatology is the same sort of thing. The evangelist feels that the traditional, futuristic eschatology is no longer meaningful.

It had been fifty years or longer since the early Christians had begun anticipating the parousia. They had thought that event was near at hand, but it was not. Each succeeding group of Christians had been disappointed. Christ had not returned again. Enough of this, the evangelist said! "Let's stop focusing attention on the future and realize that the present holds the fulfillment of those promises!" Let's use our imaginations a bit: The evangelist may have been raised in a home of Christians who looked expectantly for the imminent return of Christ. He had seen his parents die disappointed that they had not lived to witness the fulfillment of the eschatological promises. Disillusioned, the evangelist along with his fellow Christians undertook a study of these eschatological promises. What they found was that the present experience of the believers was filled with the realities looked for in the future. And so they began teaching that the present was the time of God's fulfillment of his promises. The believer already lives in the last day. Eternity is now!

This is one of the most radical revisions of traditional Christian thought the evangelist undertakes. He is saying that the Christian need not live only by hope, but by the reality of the blessings of his or her present life. He is saying that the future orientation of early Christians had deprived them of the blessedness of the present. He takes his sensual theology and expands it with an experiential eschatology. Not only is faith born out of sensual experiences, but the blessings of the future are already here to be experienced now. His is a radically present orientation—a *now* orientation. We may consider the possibility that he did not reject totally the hope for a consummation of history and all the rest. To this degree the "both and" solution described above may be partly correct. But he wanted a drastically new emphasis upon the here and now. He wanted his children not to look longingly into the future for the fulfillment of their hopes but to examine their own experience for that fulfillment.

An analogy might be found in the reaction of many persons to the space program in America. They do not reject out of hand that program. Space exploration is a legitimate and promising pursuit. But they are concerned that so much of our money is spent on the exploration of outer space while problems of our life here and now on this world increase. They say, "Let's spend more money and more energy upon the improvement of life on this planet before we devote more to the frontier of outer space." The fourth evangelist is saying that too much energy has been spent on the expectation of the future. More must be devoted to the present and the quality of Christian life here and now.

The fourth evangelist found that *the present is pregnant with possibility.* He wanted his readers to be sensitive to those possibilities and to actualize them. Eternal life? It is yours now as you live a new kind of existence on the basis of the revelation of God in Christ. Resurrection? Being born to a new kind of existence as a result of faith in Christ is resurrection. Judgment? You are judging yourself by the kind of response you make to the proclamation of the Christian gospel. Parousia? Christ comes again when you believe in him.

We recall the title of our study, "John, the Maverick Gospel." In his eschatological thought he is indeed a maverick. He runs free and unbranded. He is free of the burden of simply adhering to traditional beliefs. He is a maverick among early Christian thinkers. But unlike some mavericks, he respects and honors the past. He preserves the traditional while trying to point it in a new direction. He knew what some of the young cultural mavericks of the 1960s in America apparently did not. He knew that effective change in thought and practice does not totally disregard the past but preserves and reinterprets it. And this is precisely what he did with his eschatology.

B. THE JOHANNINE VIEW OF THE SPIRIT

But we must now begin to consider why the fourth evangelist could have such high regard for the possibilities of the present life of the Christian believer. His eschatology might be said to be the result of convictions he had about the quality of Christian experience. One of those convictions involves the presence of the Spirit among believers. Because he valued so highly the presence of the Spirit in the experience of the Christian community, he could declare that the future blessings are already present. His view of the Spirit is another of the great contributions of the fourth evangelist to Christian thought.

> *Reader's Preparation:* Below are the major passages in which the evangelist speaks of the Spirit. Read them carefully and consider these questions: Who is the Spirit? How is he related to Christ and to the Father? What does he do? Make a list of the major affirmations about the Spirit or the "Advocate." 14:15-17; 14:25-26; 15:26-27; 16:7-14.

The first thing we must do in our investigation of the pneumatology of the Fourth Gospel is to examine the peculiar word which it uses for the Spirit. That word is Paraclete (*paraklētos*). The Fourth Gospel is the only New

Testament document which uses this word to describe the Spirit. Its meaning is a bit difficult to define exactly. In effect, there are at least four different shades of meaning and hence four translations of the Greek word. The first two have in common the fact that they both come from the language of the legal court system of the day. Paraclete may mean "one called to the side of another to help." This is one who is called to assist a client in a court case. Hence, the translation, "Advocate," is used for the Greek word in the New English Bible. The second meaning is similar. The Paraclete is "one who intercedes, entreats, or makes appeals for another." Again the context is a legal trial. The Paraclete is the defense attorney (a sort of Perry Mason figure, if you will), who speaks on behalf of the defendant. Hence the translation, "Intercessor," is sometimes found in the passages you read.

The next two possible meanings of the Greek word *paraklētos* are not legal or court meanings. The first is "one who comforts and consoles another." This meaning of the Greek gave rise to the translation, "Comforter." As if this array were not enough, we find that this fascinating Greek word was also used to designate one who "proclaims or exhorts." So the word could also be appropriately translated, "Proclaimer."

Obviously the word was a very rich one in the days of our evangelist. It was one with multiple and varied meanings—witness, spokesman, consoler, and helper. The fourth evangelist seems to combine the meanings in a new way to create a new concept. We know, too, that the word was used in some Jewish circles regarding the functions of the angels. What John has done is to take this rich word and apply it to the Spirit of God. The result was an amazing theology of the Spirit. This should not surprise us. We saw in chapter one how he did essentially the same thing with the word Logos. It, too, had a wide and varied meaning. By applying it to Christ he suggested a profound and penetrating view of Christ. Much the same is true of the Spirit. With the word Paraclete he catches the imagination of a wide range of readers and opens numerous avenues of meaning for the Spirit. It is safe to say that the fourth evangelist had a way with words. Much of his genius is rooted in his capacity to use words in the most provocative manner. On that score he has as much in common with a good poet as he does with a good theologian.

Surely the application of the word Paraclete to designate the Spirit means something more. It means that for some reason the fourth evangelist was not entirely satisfied with the simple title of Spirit. Of course, he uses that expression without any apparent reservation (e.g., 3:6-8). But when he comes to the explication of the role of the Holy Spirit in chapters 14 through 16 he begins to employ the word Paraclete. Maybe he wanted to object to a common idea among the Jews that there was a special angel who functioned as the Paraclete. Maybe he wanted to affirm that it is Christ alone who gives the Spirit. And the Spirit alone is the Paraclete. On the other hand, perhaps it is the case that he simply wanted to give the Christian concept of the Spirit of God a special designation. Dealing with the leaders of the Jewish synagogue as they were, the johannine Christians needed to speak of the presence of God in their midst in a distinctive way. For whatever reason, John attaches this title to the Spirit and with his action provokes a great deal of thought.

We must try to summarize the nature and function of the Paraclete as John describes it. (Here as elsewhere in this discussion of the Paraclete I am profoundly indebted to Raymond Brown's excellent appendix on the subject in volume two of his commentary on John.) About the nature of the Paraclete we can say two things:

1. He comes from and is related to both the Father and the Son:
   a. He will come only if Jesus departs—15:26; 16:7; 16:8; 16:13.
   b. He comes from the Father—15:26.
   c. The Father gives the Paraclete as a response to Jesus' request—14:16.
   d. The Paraclete is sent in Jesus' name—14:26.
   e. Jesus sends the Paraclete from the Father—15:26 and 16:7.
2. He is identified in a number of different ways:
   a. He is called "Another Paraclete" (the implication being that Jesus is the first)—14:16.
   b. He is called the "Spirit of Truth"—14:17; 15:26; and 16:13.
   c. He is synonymous with the Holy Spirit—14:26.

In summary of the nature of the Paraclete, we may say that he is a continuation of Christ. He is the alterego of Christ. What is said of the relationship of the Son to the Father can be equally claimed of the relationship of the Paraclete to the Father. But he is dependent upon Christ's ministry as must be evident from the summary above. He is, as it were, "act two" which cannot begin until "act one" is completed.

About the function of the Paraclete we may say some things under two separate categories:

1. The relationship of the Paraclete to the disciples:
   a. They may easily recognize him—14:17.
   b. He is within and continues to remain with them—14:16-17.
   c. He is their teacher—16:13.
   d. He announces to them things which are to occur in the future—16:13.
   e. He declares what belongs to Christ and what does not—16:14.
   f. He glorifies Christ—16:14.
   g. He witnesses to Christ—15:26.
   h. He reminds the disciples of all that Jesus said—14:26.
   i. He speaks not out of himself but only what he hears—16:13.

2. The relationship of the Paraclete to the world:
   a. The world cannot accept the Paraclete—14:17.
   b. It cannot see him or recognize him—14:17.
   c. The Paraclete is rejected by the world but nonetheless witnesses to Christ amid that rejection—15:26.
   d. The Paraclete proves that the world is wrong, guilty of sin and to be condemned—16:8-11.

It is obvious that according to the Fourth Gospel the Paraclete has a two-fold function: He communicates Christ to the believers and he puts the world on trial.

As I see it, the fourth evangelist is solving two basic problems with his view of the Paraclete. The first is a problem faced by a great deal of New Testament literature, namely, the delay of the parousia. Christ has not returned as he was expected to do. But, asserts the evangelist, he has returned in the form of the Paraclete. He is present even though it seems that the parousia never occurred. The Paraclete and Christ are closely identified in the passages we have examined just so this point could be made. The Paraclete is Christ in our midst, claims the evangelist! The evangelist is showing his readers that the old Christian expectation of the return of Christ was looking in the wrong direction. Don't look into the future for the return of Christ. Look, rather, into the present experience of the community. The Christians' experience of the Spirit is their experience of the re-appeared Christ. The parousia has occurred but not in the rather gross way it was expected. Hence, the view of the Paraclete in the Gospel is part of the eschatology of the book. It is a segment of the present eschatology taught by the evangelist, and it is part of his conviction that the present experience of the believer is pregnant with possibility.

But John was also solving a much greater question with his doctrine of the Paraclete. The delay of the parousia was a peculiarly Christian problem at one stage in the history of that religion. The other problem with which John has wrestled is a much more universal concern. It is the problem of the historical distance from the time of revelation. If a religion teaches that the Ultimate Reality has revealed himself at a particular point in history, a question immediately arises. How can persons avail themselves of that revelation if they live at a later point in history? Christianity was later to come around to solving this problem by the creation of a canon. It said that the historical revelation of God is preserved in these certain writings—the Bible—and one may have access to that revelation through the reading of the Bible. But the fourth evangelist lived in a day before there was a Christian canon. His answer to the question of bridging the temporal gap back to the historical revelation is through the person and work of the Paraclete.

The Paraclete takes the revelation once made of God in the person of Jesus and mediates it to persons of a later time. This is why there is stress in the Gospel on the fact that the Paraclete does not teach *new* things but only what Christ taught (e.g., 14:26). This is why too it is asserted that the Paraclete is the witness to the revelation of God in Christ (15:26). In effect the Paraclete is the medium of divine revelation. He is the divine messenger of revelation. Let's try thinking of it this way:

GOD

PARACLETE ▬ ▬ ▬ ▬ ▬

JESUS   INDIVIDUALS

HISTORY

We can understand why this was a necessary question for the evangelist to answer. He lived in a day when the eyewitnesses of the historical Jesus were dying. There were second and even third generation Christians asking how they might have direct access to what happened some fifty years ago. John gives them their answer. They have as direct an access to that revelation as did the original disciples by virtue of the work of the Paraclete. They are not secondhand Christians. Their truth comes from an agent who is nothing less than the alter ego of Christ himself.

But there is another way of putting this—perhaps a more positive way of expressing the same concern. How is it that Christians continue to experience the presence of Christ even after all these years? Why does the revelation of God in Christ continue to grasp the lives of persons and transform them? How do we explain the reality of the presence of Christ for believers? The answer the fourth evangelist has is in his view of the Paraclete. The experience of the Christian can only be accounted for by means of the Paraclete. It is the Paraclete who is the living presence of Christ, and it is his work that keeps the revelation of God in Christ readily available to all.

The Paraclete concept is then a stroke of genius! It broke out of the limitations of the older concepts of the Spirit of God by using a new word in a new way. It gave the Christians a distinctive way of thinking of the presence of God. It answered the nagging question of the delay of the parousia. And it solved the problem of the growing temporal separation from the historical revelation. Occasionally a great thinker comes upon an idea which in a nearly perfect way speaks to his or her age. We might say that Plato, Thomas Aquinas, Hegel, Freud, and many others were such thinkers. I believe the fourth evangelist also belongs in that category, at least in terms of his concept of the Paraclete.

With the concept of the Paraclete the evangelist has again affirmed the richness of the Christian's present experience. He has declared that in that present—the now—Christ is present. The fullness of the revelation of God in history is at the individual's fingertips in the activity of the Paraclete. Eternity and history touched in the past in the incarnation of God in Christ. Eternity and history may again touch in the future as God brings history to its climactic conclusion. But eternity and history are linked in the believer's present. Eternity is now.

C. THE JOHANNINE VIEW OF THE CHURCH

The richness of the believers' present is affirmed in a still further way in what the evangelist has to say about the Christian community. It has been claimed that the concept of the church plays a minor role in the Fourth Gospel. It is even said that there is no concept of the church in this Gospel. That is claimed by virtue of the fact that the Fourth Gospel never uses the word "church." But such a judgment is premature. Without ever using the word, church, the fourth evangelist expresses a very important understanding of the Christian community. One need not use the word "love" to express a very profound sense of love in various words and actions. So, the evangelist has expressed a view of the church without ever resorting to the use of that word.

> *Reader's Preparation:* There are two allegorical speeches which are relevant to the discussion of John's view of the Christian community: (1) The Good Shepherd and the Door, 10:1-18, and (2) the True Vine, 15:1-10. Read these and then continue reading through chapters 15, 16, and 17. The heart of the concept of the Christian community is found in what Jesus is made to say in these passages regarding the relation among the Christian believers and the relation between them and Christ. See if you can draw up a list of the characteristics of these relationships.

We have claimed that there is indeed a profound view of the Christian community in the Fourth Gospel. We must, however, admit that it is a far different one than those found elsewhere in the New Testament. That is especially true if we ask about the views of the church found in the New Testament literature written after 80 A.D. From that time on in the history of the early Christian movement there was a prominent concern for the understanding of the church. There was interest in the growth of institutional matters and in the question of proper authority. Compare, for example, the passages you have just read with the Gospel of Matthew. In the latter, the nature and structure of the church is highly important. The famous (and controversial) words of Jesus spoken to Peter after the confession at Caesarea Philippi are Matthew's way of understanding the foundation of the church upon apostolic authority (Matthew 16:13-20). And Matthew's special concern for this matter can be seen when we contrast his telling of the story with those of Mark and Luke (Mark 8:27-33 and Luke 9:18-22).

This concern is not prominent in the Fourth Gospel. The whole point made by Matthew in his account of the confession at Caesarea Philippi is entirely missing in the Gospel of John. Our evangelist does not seem to have been concerned about the institutional structure of the church. His understanding of the Christian community did not focus upon the authority of the church or its leaders. Nor did he share Matthew's insistence upon the apostolic basis of the church. All this is missing from the Fourth Gospel. Why? We will suggest later that the fourth evangelist was not yet confronted with the kind of issues which drove him to an interest in institutional questions. His church is still confronting a serious threat from outside the community of believers. Hence, his view of the church is structured around that matter. Only later, when the johannine church is threatened from within by views which might undermine the community, is there a concern for institutional authority and structure. That development we see not in the Fourth Gospel but in the johannine epistles. The fourth evangelist is not really an anti-institutionalist. He just has not gotten around to the question of institutionalization!

So, what does the fourth evangelist have to say about the Christian community? We offer four generalizations about the community of believers in the Fourth Gospel. These are sweeping generalizations, to be sure, but they capture the essence of the johannine view.

First, *the community of believers is one* because of its oneness with Christ. This point is summarized in 17:23, a part of the prayer of Jesus: "That they may be one, as we are one; I in them and thou in me, may they be perfectly one." The community of believers is one with Christ. Christ is one with the Father. The members of the community are one. Here the johannine view of the community of believers builds upon its view of Christ. As there is identity and individuality between the Father and the Son, so it is with the community. The oneness spoken of in the relationship of the Christian believers with one another and with Christ is modeled after the relationship between Christ and God. The members are united with Christ, yet that does not mean they are absorbed into the being of Christ. This is not a mystical view of the community. The distinctive individuality of the community is maintained in its unity with Christ, just as the individuality of Christ is maintained in his unity with the Father.

If it is true that the relationship of the Father and Son is the model being used here, something else follows. The oneness of the believers is not a unity which abolishes individuality. They are one, but they are united as individuals. Individuality is preserved amid their commonality as members of the community. We have then the same kind of tension between individuality and identity which we confronted in chapter one when we wrestled with johannine christology. The community of believers might be analogous to the modern understanding of marriage. It is a union of two persons—"the two shall become one" (Genesis 2:24). But the individuality of the spouses is preserved. The union is real while preserving the sacredness of the distinctive persons so united. The relationship might be represented in a figure eight. If the figure is viewed one way, it is a continuous line unbroken in its unity. Viewed another way, it is two circles. Each circle is independent of the other. But they touch one another at one point. Hence, there is unity, but also distinctive individuality. Imagine, if you will, numerous figure eights all composed of one unbroken line, but forming a series of individual circles all touching upon one another. Such an imaginary figure might represent the johannine concept of the Christian community.

Second, *the community is one in love.* The theme of love among the believers is found best expressed in 15:14-17. The commandment under which the community lives is a simple one: "Love one another" (15:17). Again the model is the christological one. God loves the Son, and the Son loves the Father. The Son in turn loves the believers, and they are to love one another. The quality of the relationship between the Father and the Son and between the Father and the world (3:16) is the kind of thing to which the community is called. It is mutual love. The community of believers is to exemplify the kind of love which exists between the Father and his unique Son.

The third generalization brings us to the heart of the johannine view of the church: *The community is the locus of the manifestation of God.* This is best expressed in 17:22-23. But it involves a rather complex logic. First, it must be understood that *glory* is used here in the basic Old Testament sense of *kabōd.* That Hebrew word is used in the Old Testament to designate the manifestation of God. God is revealed, made present, in mighty deeds in history. The presence of God is glory! The logic of John's view presupposes this Old Testament foundation. The logic of the passage in chapter 17 runs like this:

Glory is given to Jesus (17:22 and 24).

Jesus gives that glory to the believers (17:22).

Therefore, the believers manifest the glory of God (17:23).

This means that the manifestation of God in Jesus has now been transferred to the community of believers. It is among them that God is made known as once he was made known in his mighty deeds in the Old Testament and then in the person and work of Christ.

This is a startling idea! It claims that the revelation of God is present in the community of Christian believers. This means that the community of believers is now what the mighty deeds of God in history and Jesus were to the world. The glory of God resides in the church! If the locus of the revelation of God was once in Jesus, it is now among and through the community of believers. If you will, the community of believers displays the continuing incarnation. The Paraclete is active among the believers, and hence it is in their midst that the presence of God is to be found.

Here is a further reason for the fourth evangelist to stress as he does the present experience of the Christian. The community of believers is the place of God's revelation, his presence. Hence, God is available to the believer in his or her present time. It is not that God will be revealed at some future time. He is, through the Paraclete, present NOW in the community. The believers are invited by the fourth evangelist to look to their present experience in the community for the revelation of God. Eternity touches history in the community of Christian believers, the evangelist boldly proclaims. So, for them, eternity is now.

We may now summarize these three generalizations about the johannine view of the community of believers. These three points are really one which we can summarize in the following diagram:

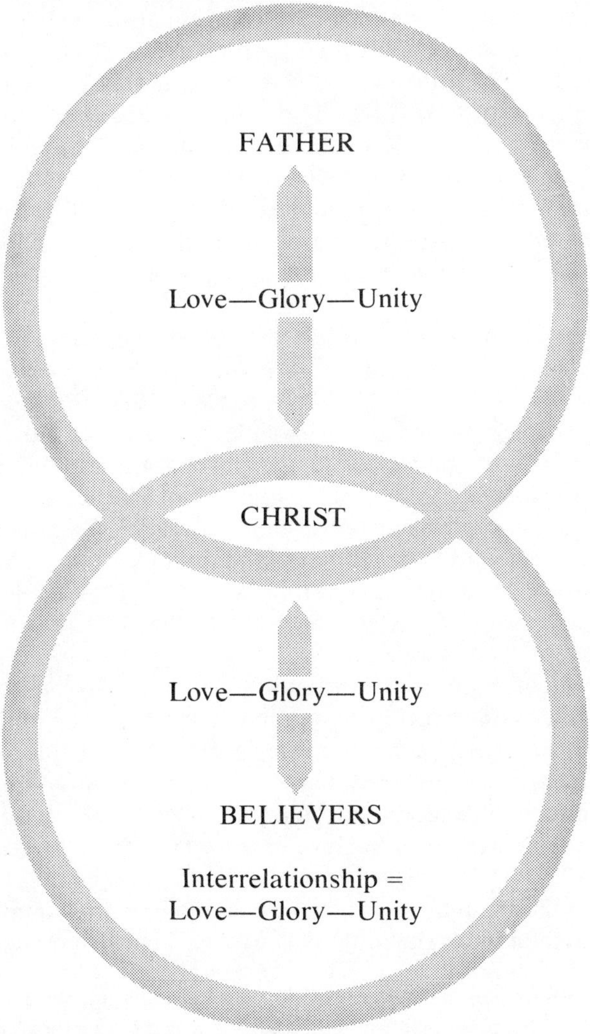

FATHER

Love—Glory—Unity

CHRIST

Love—Glory—Unity

BELIEVERS

Interrelationship =
Love—Glory—Unity

The understanding of the Christian community is shaped in the image of the relationship between the Father and the Son. As the Father loves the Son, so the believers are to love one another. As the Father and Son are united as individual beings, so the community of believers is to be united. As the Father revealed himself through the Son, so the Father reveals himself in and through the community. I submit that this is a very significant view of the church. It is one which gives a very high place to the role of the community of believers—perhaps even too high a place! It is one which values the community as the ongoing locale of that which was so decisive in the historical revelation of God in Christ.

The fourth and final generalization about the johannine view of the church is of a different kind: *The fourth evangelist "democratizes" church order.* (Here my dependence upon Ernst Käsemann is explicit. Throughout this section on the church, however, Käsemann's discussion has been a primary source.) The fourth evangelist wrote at a time when presumably the church organization was rapidly developing. However, he shows very little interest in the matter. When there is an especially high interest in early Christianity for the development of distinctive officers in the church organization, our evangelist seems to move in the opposite direction. The most striking thing about his discussion of the community of believers is that there are no distinctions made among the believers which might become a basis for official leadership. There is no distinction made between the role of the apostles (the original twelve disciples) and other believers. The fourth evangelist, as a matter of fact, does not use the expression "apostle" at all. He uses the word "disciples" where we might expect him to say "the twelve." And he seems to mean by disciple, any believer. For instance, the power to forgive sins and the gift of the Spirit are given to the disciples in general, not exclusively to the twelve (20:21-23). This led Ernst Käsemann to say that the fourth evangelist has "democratized" church order. He has de-emphasized the authority of the original followers of Jesus and claims that *all believers* have an equal authority and equal gifts. This is so, we might note, by virtue of the presence of the Spirit-Paraclete among the believers.

We are brought, then, to the difficult question of the role of Peter in the Fourth Gospel. With that question comes the role of the enigmatic "disciple whom Jesus loved" and the mysterious "other disciple." It is not just a "two for the price of one" problem we face, but a *"three* for the price of one"! We cannot solve all the problems connected with these three inter-related questions—what is the role of Peter, who is the beloved disciple and what is his role, and who is the "other disciple" and what is his role. Nor can we even take the time to summarize adequately the complexity of the questions and their interrelatedness. The following will have to suffice.

Reader's Preparation: Below are the passages in which "the disciple whom Jesus loved" is mentioned. Also, here is a list of those passages which speak of "another disciple." As you read them, you might ponder a number of questions which bear upon our immediate issue: Who was the beloved disciple? Who is this other disciple? Is the other disciple synonymous with the beloved disciple? Does the beloved disciple seem to you to be a real historical person or a symbolic figure? What is the relationship between the beloved disciple or the other disciple and Peter in those passages in which both appear? 1:37-42; 13:23-26; 18:15-16; 19:25-27; 20:2-10; 21:7 and 21:20-24.

First, a word about the role of Peter in the Fourth Gospel. It is less prominent here than in the synoptic Gospels. In our Gospel Peter simply does not emerge as the leader of the original twelve in the same way as he does in the other Gospels. Nor does he function as the sort of model disciple we are accustomed to reading about on the pages of the Synoptics. The commissioning of Peter in the passages cited above in the context of the confession at Caesarea Philippi is missing in the Fourth Gospel. The substitute story centering on Peter in chapter 21 is thought by most scholars not to have been part of the original Gospel. Chapter 21 is understood almost universally as an appendix to the Gospel, added at a later time by another author.

Second, alongside of the diminished role of Peter is the prominence of the "beloved disciple" and an unnamed disciple. The beloved disciple almost seems to take Peter's place at times. It is he who is closest to Jesus (e.g., 13:23). Peter seems to rely upon him for the meaning of Jesus' words. As Peter and "the other disciple" race to the tomb after hearing that it is empty, it is this other disciple who arrives there first (20:4). It is he who is credited with first believing that Christ had arisen from the dead (20:8).

Does this mean that the fourth evangelist wanted to depreciate the place of Peter and emphasize the prominence of another disciple? Some have argued that this is the case. They say that the evangelist is reacting against the importance assigned to Peter in the developing organization of church authority. The fourth evangelist is rebelling, they argue, against the authority of Peter. He wanted to stress that another disciple was closer to Jesus than Peter. Many scholars claim that this beloved and unnamed disciple was none other than John, the apostle, son of Zebedee, upon whose memories the Fourth Gospel is based.

Such an argument has an element of truth in it. It does seem that the fourth evangelist diminishes the prominence of Peter in favor of the beloved and unnamed disciple. But I think we need not reach the same conclusions as would some. It is not necessary to assume that the fourth evangelist is caught up in a childish game of arguing which disciple was the more important. It is not as if the fourth evangelist was saying to other Christian communities something like, "My father is more important than your father!" It is more likely, I think, that the tradition which the fourth evangelist received did not give Peter the same prominence as did the traditions embedded in the synoptic Gospels. On the other hand, the johannine tradition knew of an anonymous disciple who was highlighted in the accounts of Jesus' ministry. So, the evangelist is working with that tradition without consciously trying to depreciate one disciple and appreciate another. To put it another way, if there is an "anti-Petrine" (anti-Peter) motif in the Fourth Gospel, it is not a deliberate one. I suggest that the fourth evangelist was not aware of the growing authority of Peter in some other Christian communities. (He had not read the recent "best seller," the Gospel According to Matthew!) So, we cannot read into his Gospel a reaction against such.

But who is this mysterious beloved and unnamed disciple? There are at least three alternative answers: First, he might have been the apostle John who originated the tradition which the fourth evangelist employed. Second, he might be an ideal disciple. That is, perhaps there is no historical person represented in the figure of the beloved disciple, but only a symbol of what true Christian discipleship is all about. Third, perhaps he was a figure in the history of the johannine community who was a model disciple even though he was not an eyewitness to the historical Jesus. He was a model in much the same way Abe Lincoln is thought of as part of the spirit of America, even though Lincoln's age was nearly a century after the founding of the nation.

We would prefer to leave the mystery of the beloved disciple unsolved— partly because it may not really matter! But perhaps it is best to believe that he is a totally anonymous figure. It is difficult to maintain, I think, that he is the apostle John, son of Zebedee. And perhaps it is inappropriate to dissolve all his claim to actual historical existence, thus making him a purely symbolic character. It is true, however, that this figure *functions* in the Gospel as a symbolic ideal. That is, whether or not he was a historical person is irrelevant. What the evangelist does with him is to portray exemplary discipleship.

Sometimes in a novel one wonders if the hero is based upon some actual historical person. This is interesting to speculate about. But finally what is important is the message the novelist communicates through the hero. The question of his or her actual existence becomes insignificant. This is the case with the beloved disciple. The evangelist does not want his name known (or assumes everyone knows him already). So, what the evangelist does want to communicate is that this person is the kind of believer the reader is called to be. Furthermore, so far as church leadership is concerned, the evangelist makes no claims for the authority of this unnamed disciple. His authority is not official, not organizational. His authority is simply that he loved Jesus and was loved by his master. That authority the evangelist implies is available to any believer.

If this view of the unnamed, beloved disciple is correct, we have further evidence that the fourth evangelist holds a very democratic view of church structure and authority. The believers are all called upon to be the kind of disciple represented in the symbolic figure of the beloved disciple. Through the Paraclete all are equally capable of authoritative access to the revelation of God in Christ. The evangelist's view represents a maverick form of early Christianity once again, for he has no apparent interest in delegating special authority to special persons in the community. All believers are disciples. All believers may have that kind of relationship with Christ epitomized in the beloved disciple.

John's democratic view of church authority does not take us as far away from our central theme in this chapter as it might appear. The reason, I think, he could advance such a view of the community of believers is because of his confidence that the revelation was immediately available in the community. All persons had access through their immediate experience to the presence of God. Therefore, all were equally authorities. Because eternity is in the midst of the community's present experience, there need be no church structure or authority.

Perhaps this view of the church and church structure is naïve. Perhaps it is the view of one who has not yet seen all the problems the church must face in the world. The ideas that the community is the locus of the presence of God and that radically democratic leadership should prevail are perhaps too ideal. Did the evangelist take into account that the community could not long be as perfectly one as he imagined? Did he overlook the inevitability of splits and differences? Did he not foresee that the community would eventually embrace those who held radically different ideas? And that those ideas would need to be controlled by strong leadership? Is his view of the community of believers naïve—or, is it an expression of what the community of belief truly is? That is, perhaps he is less naïve than we think. Perhaps he is expressing the conviction that this is what the church must strive to be regardless of the circumstances it must face.

Be that as it may, John's point is made. For the fourth evangelist, the community of believers is the place where the presence of salvation is to be found. This is the evidence for his present eschatology and the reason he could take such a stand. The Paraclete in the community of faith produced an environment in which the believer's present was rich with the fulfillment of God's promise.

D. THE SACRAMENTS IN THE FOURTH GOSPEL

Here our thesis concerning the emphasis upon the believer's present experience hits a stone wall! You would expect that a Christian position like the one we have been sketching in this chapter would emphasize the sacraments, which are generally thought to be the means by which the Christian can immediately experience God's presence. Therefore, given the propensity of the fourth evangelist for an experiential theology, surely the sacraments play an important role in the Gospel. But, alas, such is not the case! At least that is not what *appears* to be the case. So, we must ask what view the evangelist did hold with regard to the sacraments.

Reader's Preparation: You are asked to read two groups of passages in preparation for the following discussion: (1) Read 1:29-39. Why does the Baptist not baptize Jesus as you now understand the Gospel? Compare 3:22 and 4:2. Read 13:1-20. This is the point in the narrative where one would expect (from the synoptic pattern) to find the institution of the Lord's Supper. Does the washing of the feet of the disciples function as a substitute for the Last Supper sacrament? Is it a sacrament? (2) The following are passages in the Fourth Gospel which are sometimes understood to be references to the sacraments of the Lord's Supper and Baptism. Read them and determine for yourself whether or not references to the sacraments are intended. 2:1-11; 3:5; 6:1-13; 6:51-59; 13:1-17; 15:1-6; and 19:34.

The first thing that strikes one about the Fourth Gospel when the question of the sacraments is posed is one simple fact: The institutions of the sacraments are missing! Jesus himself is not baptized. His baptism has been the traditional sanction for the rite of Baptism in Christian practice. And from the Fourth Gospel we cannot even discern clearly if Jesus practiced baptism! At one point it is said that he did and at another that he did not (3:22 and 4:2). Neither does Jesus institute the Last Supper or Eucharist! Such blatant omissions put into question any sort of discussion of sacramentality in the Fourth Gospel. It is like asking if the Wright brothers believed in space travel! There is simply no explicit mention of the sanctions of the two rites of Baptism and the Lord's Supper.

But some scholars find explicit reference to the sacraments at other points in the Gospel. They argue that the transformation of the water into wine in the story of the wedding at Cana implies the wine of the Eucharist. Jesus' assertion that one must be born "from water and spirit" in 3:5 is, say some, a sure allusion to Baptism. Moreover, the feeding of the multitude in chapter 6 is understood by many to be the johannine institution of the Last Supper. There (v. 11) Jesus gives thanks and distributes the bread and fish. The Greek word translated "gave thanks" is *eucharistēsas*. That Greek word is the root of the word Eucharist. The eucharistic meaning of the feeding of the crowd is made explicit, say these interpreters, in the speech of Jesus coming later in the chapter (vv. 51-58). There Jesus is made to declare, "Unless you eat the flesh of the Son of Man and drink his blood you can have no life in you." (v. 53) Others find the washing of the feet of the disciples in chapter 13 to be a symbolic representation of the meaning of the Eucharist. Perhaps the allegory of the vine (15:1-6) is meant to imply the eucharistic wine. Finally, 19:34 speaks of the blood and water flowing from Jesus' side. The blood may represent the eucharistic cup and the water, Baptism, according to some interpreters.

Consequently, in spite of the absence of the institutions of the sacraments, some scholars argue that the fourth evangelist is highly appreciative of the sacraments. The point is, they argue, that he took for granted his reader's understanding of the institutions of the sacraments. Therefore, he focuses upon their meaning, particularly in chapters 6 and 13. This understanding of the evangelist claims that he was a sacramentarian of the highest kind. In this case, silence is understood as profound appreciation rather than neglect. The poet who wishes to celebrate the Bicentennial in a work does not rehearse the history of the founding of these United States. Rather, he alludes perhaps subtly to the depths of meaning in the spirit of those founding events. So, too, argue some, did the fourth evangelist celebrate the significance of the Lord's Supper and Baptism.

But there are those who would propose a drastically different alternative. Bultmann and others have argued that the fourth evangelist was an anti-sacramentarian. He knew of the sacraments, but was disgusted by their abuse in the church of his time. So, he deliberately ignored them in his Gospel. His silence was a loud protest against the sacraments! The water of Baptism and the bread and wine of the Eucharist had come to take the place of Christ himself, the evangelist thought. But his Gospel eventually was revised. This view is part of the "spoiler" theory described above in the section on eschatology. A rather traditional-thinking churchman read the Gospel. He did not like, among other things, the omission of any reference to the sacraments. So, he went through and added sacramental passages at points such as 3:5 (by inserting the words, "water and") and 6:51-58. The result is that these passages stand out like sore thumbs in the otherwise anti-sacramental Gospel.

A third view of the sacraments in the Fourth Gospel is that our evangelist was a revisionist. That is, he did not oppose the sacraments (as Bultmann would have us believe), nor did he endorse them (as proponents of the first alternative would counsel). Rather, what he wanted to do was to revise our understanding of them. So, the footwashing scene interprets the meaning of the sacrament of the Lord's Supper as does chapter 6. Baptism is interpreted as a meaningful rebirth only along with the gift of the Spirit in 3:5.

Still a fourth alternative for understanding the sacraments in the Fourth Gospel goes something like this: John did not mean to ignore the sacraments in his Gospel. Rather, he left them at an implicit level rather than explicit. Gradually, the Gospel underwent small revisions which sought to make the sacramental references more explicit. Baptism was surely implied in the discussion of chapter 3, so some kindly reviser added the words, "water and" to make the meaning of the passage clearer. This view differs from the "spoiler" theory of Bultmann and his followers in an important way. The revisers who are responsible for many of the sacramental passages are in agreement with, rather than opposition to, the evangelist's view. They are helping him say more clearly what they know he wanted to say.

Finally, a bold alternative remains. It is to suggest that the evangelist did not know the tradition of the sacraments. The evangelist had no access to the stories of the origin of the sacraments and his Christian community did not observe them. This was possible because the johannine church was out of the mainstream of early Christian development (that is, the development known to us through the Pauline epistles and the synoptic Gospels). He was not a sacramentarian or an anti-sacramentarian. He was rather asacramental—meaning he was ignorant of the sacraments and the traditions about them. Such a view is possible only if you take seriously a couple of assumptions. First, that the johannine community was not tied closely with the other Christian communities of the time. If the johannine community did not know the synoptic Gospels and the epistles of Paul, they were a relatively isolated Christian church. Second, that their isolation was due in part to the fact that they were for years a Christian community within the synagogue. They lived, as it were, within the confines of the Jewish community and were for that reason non-sacramental. The result was, as we have claimed several times, a maverick Christianity.

If this last alternative is indeed the case, then the references which are often argued to be sacramental must be read differently. References to "gave thanks" and "eat flesh" are not eucharistic. Every time the evangelist mentions wine or water he does not intend that his readers should think of the sacraments. (Just because syncopation is typical of popular rock music does not mean that wherever there is syncopation that is rock—quite the contrary!) So, the evangelist could well use words which were elsewhere in the Christian movement associated with the sacraments without meaning to suggest sacramental meaning. It could well be that some of the sacramental sounding passages were later additions to the Gospel. After the Gospel was in circulation in the wider Christian community, perhaps words and phrases were added to refer to the sacraments. This is especially the case in 3:5 where a strong argument can be made that the words, "water and," were not in the original text. But such additions were not in opposition to the evangelist's view. Nor were they friendly revisions to make explicit what the evangelist implied. They were additions at a point where the evangelist was neutral.

I believe that this last alternative offers us the best explanation of the evangelist's view of the sacraments. It explains the evidence the best, it seems to me, and fits neatly into the emerging view of the Gospel as a document written by a Christian group not associated with the wider Christian community. But the point of our section is not to propagate this view of the evangelist and the Christian sacraments. It is rather to find another dimension to the evangelist's emphasis upon the fulfillment of salvation in the present.

It is time to recall a point made earlier in chapter three. There we proposed that the evangelist's "sensory theology" is really quite sacramental. That is, the suggestion that faith grows out of immediate, everyday physical experiences is precisely what the sacraments in Christian thought are all about. When the evangelist asserts that seeing and hearing are the beginnings of the growth of faith, he is proposing a sacramentality, for the sacraments are sensuous experiences which are supposed to epitomize the presence of God in ordinary realities. Bread and wine and water become the sensory experiences through which the Ultimate Reality is communicated to the believer in his or her present situation. So, the evangelist's view of the relationship of faith and experience is fundamentally a sacramental view, I propose. Consequently, had the evangelist known of the sacraments he might well have appreciated them as he appreciated the signs as sensory beginnings of the growth of faith. And without knowing of them he conceived a theology which is remarkably congenial to them. He would, however, never allow that the sacraments alone are the sensory experiences which nurture faith. He would have wanted to say, I think, that they are the epitomization of the manner in which normal experience is related to faith.

Drawn back to the evangelist's view of the relationship of faith and experience, we can see even more clearly, I hope, how he believed that the Christians' present experience was ripe with the actualization of God's salvation. Whatever his view of the sacraments themselves, he seems clearly to have honored the present as the time of salvation. Eternity touches history in the experience of the believer *now*.

E. CONCLUSION

If the exposition just completed is at all true to the Gospel, we have a remarkably consistent picture. The experience of the Paraclete, the understanding of the church, and the evangelist's view of experience and faith all fit neatly together. They form the foundation upon which the fourth evangelist could assert his radical present eschatology. They are the axioms of his system. And they all lead to one conclusion: God is present in the believer's experience. He is known now. His gifts of salvation are immediately available. We might put it this way in order to summarize all of this:

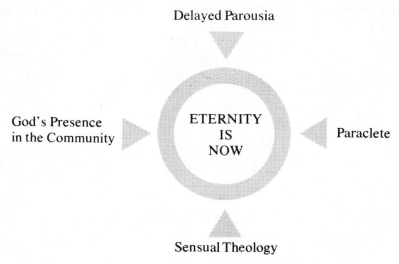

Delayed Parousia

God's Presence in the Community

ETERNITY IS NOW

Paraclete

Sensual Theology

These elements all feed into the conviction that the present time is the time of salvation. Each one drives the evangelist toward his radical present eschatology and away from a focus upon the future.

This constitutes a bold solution to the religious problem posed in the introduction to this chapter. Are the benefits of religious salvation available in the believers' present experience or only in the future? The fourth evangelist confidently asserts that it is now that the believer knows those benefits. And he claims this on the basis of his own experience and that of his community. He does not deny the future and the hope for what the future will bring. But he apparently believes that the future holds no surprises for the Christians, for they already experience the future in their present. God's benefits for humanity are not confined to a blessed past. Nor is it that there will be ''pie in the sky by and by.'' *Now* is the time for the bestowal of those gifts for which all humanity yearns.

The evangelist's view makes logical sense the way we have laid it out. There is a consistency between his experience and his conclusions. That is admirable. Whether or not his view of the matter is universally true is a far more difficult task. Did he and his community correctly understand their experience? Or did they deceive themselves? Did he put too much emphasis upon the present? Was he overreacting to Chrisitan futuristic eschatology (like an adolescent might overreact to the views of her or his parents on a particular issue)? These are questions I leave in your hands to ponder and discuss.

It needs only to be said that the evangelist structured a view which made sense out of his experience. That is what all human beings must do as best they can: determine the meaning of their experience and found their religious beliefs (whatever they may be) upon that determination. If the fourth evangelist is wrong in terms of his conclusions about the presence of eternity in the now, at least his is an example of the way in which the task of seeking a religious position must be done.

Conclusion: John, the Universal Gospel

A FEW YEARS AGO there was much talk in America about the generation gap and about the rebellion of youth. Gradually what came to our attention was the fact that almost every age in the history of the human race had experienced a degree of the same thing. Young people were separated from their parents by a different view of the world, different priorities, different ideas, and different goals. Communication between parents and their young adult children was strained and problematic. Such a situation, we learned, was not the exclusive property of the 1960s in America. It could be found as far back as ancient Greece. Youthful rebels are in many ways a universal phenomenon.

I would like us to bring our discussion of the thought and symbolism of the Fourth Gospel to a close with this proposal: The Fourth Gospel is in many ways a maverick piece of first century Christian literature—a rebel. It strikes out in a drastically different direction from that of the other New Testament writings. At the same time, beneath the basic concerns of the Gospel, as we have formulated them, lie some universal religious questions. The questions the fourth evangelist deals with in his document are questions not confined to first century Christianity. They are questions which many religious traditions have pondered and continue to ponder. So, the Fourth Gospel viewed in one context is a maverick Gospel, a rebel. But viewed in a wider context it is a universal Gospel. Let's conclude our survey of the Gospel by considering these two different views of the work—a maverick Gospel, a universal Gospel.

A. THE PLACE OF JOHANNINE THOUGHT
AND SYMBOLISM IN EARLY CHRISTIANITY

We have argued from the beginning that the Fourth Gospel represents a peculiar form of first century Christian thought. This is a dangerous argument, because it could be made with regard to any piece of New Testament writing. It can be argued for instance that the Gospel of Luke and the Acts of the Apostles are a form of Christian thought quite different from the Gospels of Mark and Matthew and clearly distinct from Pauline Christianity. A similar case could be made for other sections of the New Testament. But the contention of this introduction to the Fourth Gospel is that with johannine Christianity one is dealing with a more fundamental uniqueness. Luke was dependent upon Mark and probably the hypothetical source of sayings called "Q". So was Matthew. While Luke may have misunderstood Paul, he claimed to represent the early apostle accurately. John makes no claim of being linked with other forms of early Christianity, and there is good evidence that this was indeed the case.

We may speak of the uniqueness of johannine Christianity under several categories. The first is the uniqueness of the *tradition* embedded in the Gospel. As we suggested in the Introduction, that tradition was an independent stream of Christian thought. It must have rooted in an oral tradition which also eventually gave rise to the synoptic traditions. But it was distinct both in form and content. The evangelist faithfully preserves that tradition which his community knew and cherished. His preservation of traditional materials has struck us again and again in the course of our study. The fact that he preserved these particular traditions sets his Gospel apart from the other early Christian literature. And it is the Fourth Gospel alone, so far as we know, that informs us of the existence of that non-synoptic, non-Pauline tradition.

Second, we may speak of the uniqueness of the johannine *situation*. While all early Christianity may be traced back to Jewish roots, the Fourth Gospel is different. The earliest Christians were all Jewish Christians. They were related to their Jewish heritage while at the same time adhering to their new Christian beliefs. But very soon the Christians stood independent of Judaism. Already in the writings of the Apostle Paul that split is well under way. Paul finds his most promising candidates for the Christian faith not amid his fellow Jews but among the Gentiles. We assume that the split of Gentile Christians from the Jewish Christians was solid by the so-called Jerusalem Council, *ca.* 49 A.D. The independence of Christianity from Judaism was surely completed by the early 60s and certainly by the destruction of Jerusalem in 70 A.D.

But in the Gospel of John we find that the split from the synagogue is a much more recent phenomenon. Everything we have encountered in this study has pointed to the fact that the fourth evangelist was dealing with a community recently expelled from the synagogue and engaged in a serious dialogue with the Jewish leaders. One is almost tempted to say that the johannine church was slow in coming out of the womb of Judaism! It had lived peacefully there amid the Jewish adherents for years longer than other Christian communities. Dare we say that in comparison with the other Christian communities it was slower in its development? Is the johannine church like the young woman who continues to live with her parents until the age of thirty-five and only then is expelled from her home? The analogy works only so far. It is true that johannine Christianity lived longer in the safety of the Jewish synagogue. But it does not seem to have been the case that such safety retarded its development. For the tradition preserved in the Fourth Gospel suggests that it had a long history and had been carefully nurtured. Certainly we cannot say that the fourth evangelist himself was a less mature Christian!

Now, however, the johannine community finds itself cast out of the synagogue. The result, we have suggested, was a serious and traumatic social dislocation. The crisis affected the identity of the Christians in that community. Who were they if not Jews who embraced Christ? What is their Christianity if not a refined and sophisticated Judaism of a particular kind? Like the young adult who is disowned by his parents, the johannine community was in the midst of an identity crisis. This crisis was made worse by the continuing conflict with the Jewish synagogue. This situation contributes significantly to the distinctiveness of the Fourth Gospel and its thought.

We may speak of the distinctiveness of the Fourth Gospel in terms of its tradition and in terms of its situation. But finally we may speak of that distinctiveness in terms of its *thought and symbolism*. The uniqueness of johannine thought and symbolism is a result in part of the first two categories. The tradition employed by the fourth evangelist makes the concepts and symbolism of his work distinctive. The situation in which and for which he is writing likewise contributes to that distinctiveness of thought and language. However, we must add that the genius of the evangelist himself plays a major role in the unique form of Christianity which he embraced. I hope that the previous chapters have demonstrated again and again how the mind of the evangelist worked in a decisively distinct way. To cite but one example, we may recall his fondness for reshaping pregnant words for his own use. The concepts of the Logos and the Paraclete are both built upon that fondness. He took rich words and molded them to a new Christian use.

We need rehearse only briefly and generally some of the uniqueness of the thought and symbolism of the Fourth Gospel. First, the unique view of Christ as the Father's Son stands out. Nowhere in the New Testament do we find a christology shaped in quite this manner. The evangelist tried to hold together the unity and individuality of the Father and the Son. The "I am" sayings contribute to his christology and distinguish his view of Christ from others in the New Testament.

Second, his dualism is more pronounced than any we can find in the other early Christian literature. The blend of a human dualism and a cosmic dualism is different. Different too is his use of a wide variety of terms to express the poles of the dualism. Similarly, I would maintain that no New Testament writing wrestles so consciously with the question of divine determinism and human freedom as does the fourth evangelist. However, I will concede that Paul runs a close second!

Third, the evangelist's experiential theology stands out. Nowhere in the New Testament can we find a concept of the relationship of faith and experience worked out as thoroughly as in the Fourth Gospel. Nowhere is the sensual basis of faith emphasized as it is here. But equally distinct is the insistence of the Fourth Gospel that faith without seeing and hearing is the goal of the believer. Faith and knowledge are explicated in a manner unlike other early Christian thinkers.

Finally, the emphasis upon the presence of salvation in the believers' experience significantly departs from the common themes of other New Testament literature. While the effort to solve the problem of the delay of the parousia is beneath the surface of a number of pieces of New Testament literature, they do not offer a solution as radical as that of the fourth evangelist. The profound appreciation for the believers' present is clearly distinct. We could go on to mention his peculiar concept of the Spirit-Paraclete, the church, and his treatment of the sacraments. But we will let this be enough to jog the reader's memory.

The distinctiveness of johannine thought and symbolism is clear, I hope. Yet it should not be overly stressed. Perhaps that is the danger our discussion has run. One may itemize the way in which two sisters are so radically different. They embrace entirely different lifestyles. They do not even have a "family resemblance" about their physical appearance. They diverge in their talents and skills. One wonders how they could even be sisters. Yet they are. And when the analysis goes far enough the family heritage is evident. Different though they are, they are genetically similar. They share the same parents. So, our analysis of the distinctiveness of the Fourth Gospel must recognize that it shares the same genetic structure with other forms of Christianity in the first century. It has the same parentage with other New Testament writings. It too roots in the witnesses to the man Jesus of Nazareth and the earliest community of believers gathered about belief in him. Maybe the distinctiveness of the Fourth Gospel results from the environment which shaped it after its birth. Maybe too the difference between the two sisters might be traced to differences in their environment.

How then shall we characterize the place of johannine thought and symbolism in early Christianity? We have utilized the expression, maverick Gospel. And that seems most fitting, for the thought and symbolism of the Gospel does not seem to strain for consistency with any other form of early Christian thought. Rather, it freely goes its own way and explores new avenues of expression. It is an adventuresome Christianity, one might say. It does not flow with the mainstream of New Testament thought. But still it must be stressed that it is *Christian*. It shares with the rest of the New Testament the basic Christian gospel. So, a maverick it may be in the context of the New Testament. But it shares with the rest of the canonical literature a profound commitment to the belief that God has acted decisively in the person of Jesus for the salvation of humanity.

It is instructive to look ahead in the history of New Testament Christianity, beyond the production of the Gospel itself. The three Epistles which carry the name of John in the canon may help us to understand the place of the Fourth Gospel in relationship with early Christianity. It appears that the johannine Epistles were all written at a later time than the Gospel. They were composed after johannine Christianity seems to have become associated more closely with the mainstream of early Christian thought.

They were written, at least in part, to stem the tide of a heretical movement in the johannine church. That heretical movement appears to be based upon the Fourth Gospel! It appears that there were some in the later johannine church who were taking the Fourth Gospel very seriously. The results were that they were out of line with the direction of their church. The author (or authors) of the three Epistles were concerned to bring these wanderers back into the fold. The fold was an orthodox church built upon the Fourth Gospel and its tradition, but now harmonized with the mainstream of early Christian thought.

But note what it is that the Epistles are concerned to correct in these heretics. The eschatology of 1 John stresses the nearness of the parousia (2:18ff. and 2:28–3:2). It emphasizes the reality of the humanity of Jesus against a christology which apparently did not take the incarnation as seriously as it should (1 John 4:2 and 2:22 and 2 John 7). It stresses the fact of human sin because the rebels did not seem sufficiently conscious of their own sin (1 John 1:8ff.). The Epistles then were written by those who believed johannine Christianity to be fully homogeneous with mainstream orthodox Christianity. They wanted these radical thinkers corrected. As J.L. Houlden points out, the johannine Epistles "are all part of a campaign to put a brake upon those who would 'gnosticize' the johannine tradition of Christian teaching." (*The Johannine Epistles,* p. 18. Houlden does an excellent job of relating the Gospel and the Epistles in his commentary.)

The Fourth Gospel was, then, a most likely candidate for a document in which a heretical movement could find inspiration. We do not contend that the heretics attacked in the johannine Epistles correctly interpreted the Gospel. The opposite is generally the case, I think. But the fact that a heretical movement grew out of the johannine community on the basis of the Fourth Gospel is most important. The "gnostic" movement of the second century within the Christian church found the Fourth Gospel most congenial to its ideas. This was the case, I suggest, because the Gospel was not a "standard" Christian document. It was different. It allowed for the possibilities of heretical interpretations. Examples—its dualism, its deterministic passages, and its christology. This historical fact of the susceptibility of the Fourth Gospel to heretical interpretation makes our point. It is an unusual piece of first century Christian literature. Ernst Käsemann has called the theology of the fourth evangelist a "naïve gnosticism." I do not think that is entirely correct. But I think there is a sense in which the fourth evangelist writes with a naïve disregard of how his ideas and symbols may fit into the emerging pattern of early Christian thought. His is an unbranded Gospel—a maverick. He does not seem to care about "fitting in." He simply speaks his mind—preserving the traditions he knows and addressing as effectively as possible the community he has in mind.

There is something refreshing and exciting about that. And it is that very feature of the Fourth Gospel that makes its study all the more intriguing.

B. JOHANNINE THOUGHT AND SYMBOLISM AS
REPRESENTATIVE OF THE RELIGIOUS QUEST

How then can we entitle this conclusion to our study, "John, the Universal Gospel"? Its relationship with other early Christian thought seems to necessitate that it is a very particular Gospel, designed for and written out of a very special occasion. Hardly universal!

Yet the other theme of our study has been to show how the Fourth Gospel in its peculiar way deals with some of the basic questions in the religious quest of humans. We have tried to relate the major ideas in johannine thought to major questions which one finds in a number of religions. We have shown that broad, almost universal questions have been addressed in the thought of the maverick Gospel. Let's review the ones we have touched upon in the course of our study:

First, there is the question of *the nature of the founder of the religious movement.* Every religion must come to some definition of the nature and work of its founder. Each religious tradition gradually works through this question. Finally, a mature, established religion settles upon some statement regarding its founder. In its christology the Fourth Gospel makes a daring effort to do just that with regard to Jesus of Nazareth. In his claim that Jesus was the Father's Son, the fourth evangelist works through the statement of the nature and work of the founder of the Christian movement.

Second, what is *the nature and source of evil*—that which opposes and frustrates the will of God? Again, this is a universal question in religion. Every religion poses an answer, some more clearly than others, some more insistently than others. But always the religious system must take account of the reality of the undesirable aspect of life. The fourth evangelist (perhaps unconsciously) does just this in his provocative dualism. Whatever the problems may be in understanding the nature of that dualism, it is his answer to the reality of evil. It is that dualistic split among persons which the divine will seeks to overcome. It is the negative pole of that dualism which accounts for the reality of the resistence to belief.

Third, *the relationship of faith to experience* haunts every religious thinker. How is experience to be understood in relationship with religious belief? Is faith based on experience? If so, how? Such questions are not limited to Christian thought or even to western religious mentality. They are universal religious concerns. Our evangelist has explored and probed those questions rather thoroughly. The result is that beneath the surface of his Gospel rests a very profound concept of the relationship of faith and experience.

Fourth, religions promise some sort of salvation—some benefit for humans. The question is whether that benefit is bestowed in the believers' earthly existence or promised for some future age or abode. The religious question of *the relationship of the present and the future in the promise of salvation* is perhaps an expression of a broader philosophical question.

Maybe the religious question expresses the philosophical concern for the threefold existence of time—past, present, and future. Regardless of that matter, concern for the present and the future bestowal of the benefits of belief smolders in every religious tradition. In his strong effort to highlight the present time of salvation, the fourth evangelist offers a solution to that universal religious question. He dares to declare out of the experience of his community that for Christians eternity is now.

The fact that the fourth evangelist deals with these four universal religious questions is our reason for claiming that John is a universal Gospel. Hence, we do not mean necessarily that the Fourth Gospel offers a religious system of thought and practice which every person in every age can embrace in detail. Perhaps a case for that claim could be made. But we are not concerned with it here. The point is that the fourth evangelist shows us how a religious community wrestles with at least four (and doubtless many more) questions that concern every religious person in nearly every age. In that sense his is a universal Gospel.

An illustration from another area of early Christian literature might help. The Book of Revelation and the writings of Karl Marx have a good deal in common. Both the author of Revelation (John of Patmos) and Marx deal with a universal religious question: What is the meaning of history? Each of them proposes a view of history and its meaning. Both try to evoke their readers' belief that their view of history is true. They deal with a basic human question. All thoughtful persons ask themselves, ''What is history all about?'' Is it just a pointless sequence of occurrences leading nowhere? Is there a pattern to the events of history? Do humans alone determine the course of history? Or, is there some outside force which determines, or at least shapes, the general direction of history? John of Patmos and Marx give radically different answers to these questions, but both propose solutions. They both undertake to respond to a universal yearning of the human mind to understand history. The Fourth Gospel is universal in that it addresses itself to a number of such questions. It reaches beyond its parochial setting to embrace universal inquiries which arise from humans in quest for religious understanding.

Maybe our point could be put this way: It is not the content of the thought of the Gospel but its method that is universal. It is the way in which the fourth evangelist addresses himself to these matters. It is his effort to resolve the issues haunting the religious person. Perhaps not his solutions, but his questions make the fourth evangelist a universal thinker. So, it might be that his solutions to the questions are less relevant than his willingness to pose the questions. His answers may be less applicable than his questions!

Sometimes a teacher is remembered by her pupils for years. But often it is not *what* she taught, but *how* she taught that makes such a lasting impression. The fourth evangelist is perhaps a universal thinker not by virtue of *what* he thought but *how* he thought. He is an example for every religious person in this way. He exemplifies the necessity of facing certain issues honestly and directly.

Some would want to make a much different kind of claim for the universality of the Gospel. I would not deny their right to do so. But for now I want us to become aware of this first level of universalism in the Gospel— the level of the questions it poses.

Finally, then, the Fourth Gospel is *a maverick Gospel* in the context of early Christianity. Yet it is one which deals with important issues in the lives of religious persons of many different persuasions in many different centuries. It represents the diversity of early Christian thought and the universality of the basic questions connected with being religious. Thus it is both a maverick and *a universal Gospel*.

It is my understanding that for years after the first performance of Beethoven's Ninth Symphony ("The Choral Symphony"), the finale of that work was a storm center for critics. They hotly debated Beethoven's drastic departure from the usual symphonic form. The theme of the final movement was either judged an utter failure, or else it was hailed as a brilliant stroke of genius. Critics were widely divided on the question. It appeared that one was either convinced of the final movement's depravity of artistic success or of its unprecedented brilliance.

Often genius is hard to detect from drastic failure. The genius in his or her own age is often taken for an idiot, and some who are hailed as geniuses are proven by history to have been idiots. So it is with the fourth evangelist. We must either say that his work is brilliant—a stroke of genius—or a regrettable mistake in early Christian thought. There seems to be little middle ground. The question, I suppose, can only be resolved by each student in the light of his or her own convictions. Still, this much we can agree upon: The Fourth Gospel represents an intriguing and provocative piece of religious literature. It is one which bears our study again and again. Whether genius or blunderer, the fourth evangelist invites our analysis and tantalizes our minds with his ideas and his language. He has done so for centuries and will doubtless continue to do so for centuries to come.

Bibliography

The works listed below are a few of the important studies which might be recommended to the student of John. They are listed here for two reasons: First, they are the ones upon which this book depends most heavily. Second, they are the ones to which the reader should go to pursue issues raised in this book.

Barrett, C.K. *The Gospel According to St. John.* London: SPCK, 1958.

Brown, Raymond E. *The Gospel According to John.* The Anchor Bible, volumes 29 and 29a. New York: Doubleday & Co., 1966, 1970. Two volumes. (The best commentary on the Fourth Gospel!)

Bultmann, Rudolf. *The Gospel of John.* Philadelphia: Westminster Press, 1971. (Obviously a modern classic!)

———.*The Theology of the New Testament.* New York: Charles Scribner's Sons, 1955. Volume Two.

Dodd, C.H. *The Interpretation of the Fourth Gospel.* Cambridge: University Press, 1963.

———.*Historical Tradition in the Fourth Gospel.* Cambridge: University Press, 1963.

Fortna, Robert T. *The Gospel of Signs.* Cambridge: University Press, 1970.

———."From Christology to Soteriology. A Redaction-Critical Study of Salvation in the Fourth Gospel." *Interpretation,* 27 (1973), pp. 32-45.

Fuller, Reginald H. *The Foundations of New Testament Christology.* New York: Charles Scribner's Sons, 1965.

Harner, Philip B. *The "I Am" of the Fourth Gospel.* Philadelphia: Fortress Press, 1970.

Houlden, J.L. *The Johannine Epistles.* Harper's New Testament Commentary. New York: Harper & Row, 1973. (The best introduction to the johannine Epistles!)

Käsemann, Ernst. *The Testament of Jesus According to John 17.* Philadelphia: Westminster Press, 1968.

Kee, Howard Clark. *The Origins of Christianity: Sources and Documents.* Englewood Cliffs, N.J.: Prentice-Hall, Inc., 1973.

King, Winston L. *Introduction to Religion: A Phenomenological Approach.* New York: Harper & Row, 1968.

Kysar, Robert. *The Fourth Evangelist and His Gospel.* Minneapolis: Augsburg Publishing House, 1975.

Martyn, J. Louis. *History and Theology in the Fourth Gospel.* New York: Harper & Row, 1968.

Meeks, Wayne A. "The Man from Heaven in Johannine Sectarianism." *Journal of Biblical Literature,* 91 (1972), pp. 44-72.

Perrin, Norman. *The New Testament: An Introduction.* New York: Harcourt Brace Jovanovich, Inc., 1974.

Robinson, J.A.T. "The Most Primitive Christology of All?" *Twelve New Testament Studies.* Naperville, Ill.: Alec Allenson, 1962, pp. 139-153.

Schnackenburg, Rudolf. *The Gospel According to St. John.* New York: Herder and Herder, 1968. Volume One.

Vanderlipp, D. George. *Christianity According to John.* Philadelphia: Westiminster Press, 1975.